Computer Operations Management

IT Infrastructure Library

Gildengate House, Upper Green Lane
Norwich NR3 1DW

LONDON: HMSO

© Copyright: Controller of Her Majesty's Stationery Office, 1990

First published: 1990

ISBN: 0 11 330539 7

This is one of the books in the IT Infrastructure Library series. At regular intervals, further books will be published and the Library will be completed by late 1991. Since many customers would like to receive the IT Infrastructure Library books automatically on publication, a standing order service has been set up. For further details on standing orders please contact:

HMSO Publicity(P9D), FREEPOST, Norwich, NR3 1BR
(*No stamp needed for UK customers*).

Until the whole Library is published, and subject to availability, draft copies of unpublished books may be obtained from CCTA if you are a standing order customer. To obtain drafts please contact:

IT Infrastructure Management Services, CCTA, Gildengate House, Upper Green Lane, Norwich, NR3 1DW.

For further information on other CCTA products, contact:

Press and Public Relations, CCTA, Riverwalk House, 157-161 Millbank, London, SW1P 4RT.

This document has been produced using procedures conforming to BSI 5750 Part 1: 1987; ISO 9001: 1987.

HUMBERSIDE LIBRARIES

Table of contents

	Foreword	vii
1.	**Management summary**	1
2.	**Introduction**	3
2.1	Purpose	3
2.2	Target readership	3
2.3	Scope	3
2.4	Related guidance	4
2.5	Standards	7
3.	**Planning for computer operations management**	9
3.1	Procedures	9
3.1.1	The Operations Manager	9
3.1.2	Service Level Requirements	12
3.1.3	Computer installation and acceptance	13
3.1.4	Operations interface with other IT infrastructure management activities	15
3.1.5	Operability standards and the move to advanced ops	19
3.1.6	Accepting and running applications software	22
3.1.7	Operations and the people interface	25
3.1.8	Computer operations	28
3.1.9	Security	55
3.1.10	Measuring Operations' efficiency and effectiveness	58
3.1.11	Management reviews and audits	65
3.2	Dependencies	65
3.2.1	Hardware and software tools	65
3.2.2	Documentation	66
3.2.3	Accommodation	69
3.2.4	Adapting to change	72
3.3	People	74
3.3.1	Staffing	74
3.3.2	Organization	77
3.3.3	Training	82
3.4	Timing	85

4.	**Implementation**		**87**
4.1	Procedures		87
4.1.1	Informing staff and users		87
4.1.2	Install and implement hardware and software tools		88
4.1.3	Test Ops procedures		89
4.1.4	Implement budgetary control		89
4.1.5	Support affected staff		90
4.1.6	Finalize arrangements for out-of-hours working		90
4.1.7	Put the procedures into effect		90
4.1.8	Cope with implementation problems		90
4.1.9	Ensure adherence to procedures		91
4.2	Dependencies		91
4.3	Staff		92
4.4	Timing		92
5.	**Post-implementation and audit**		**93**
5.1	Procedures		93
5.1.1	Post-implementation review		93
5.1.2	The Operations Manager - performance reviews		94
5.1.3	Efficiency and effectiveness reviews and management checks		94
5.1.4	User involvement in reviewing Ops		100
5.1.5	Audits		100
5.1.6	External consultant reviews		102
5.2	Dependencies		103
5.3	Staff		103
5.3.1	Organization		103
5.3.2	Management of staff		104
5.4	Timing		105
6.	**Benefits, costs and possible problems**		**107**
6.1	Benefits		107
6.2	Costs		108
6.3	Possible problems		108

Table of contents

7.	**Tools**	**109**
7.1	Schedulers	109
7.2	Magnetic tape and data cartridge management systems	111
7.3	Disk management systems	113
7.4	JCL validation and management systems	114
7.5	Job documentation systems	115
7.6	Output and distribution systems	115
7.7	Console operator automation systems	117

Annexes

A.	**Glossary of terms**	**A1**
B.	**Example - Job descriptions**	**B1**
B.1	Ops Manager	B1
B.2	Shift Leader	B2
B.3	Senior Operator/Operator	B3
B.4	Junior/Trainee Operator	B4
B.5	Operations Analyst	B4
B.6	Data Control Clerk	B5
B.7	Media Librarian	B6
B.8	Systems Programmer	B7
C.	**Example - Operations manual contents**	**C1**
D.	**Example - Staff access levels/zones**	**D1**
E.	**Example - Procedures for handling cheques/secure items**	**E1**

The IT Infrastructure Library
Computer Operations Management

Foreword

*Welcome to the IT Infrastructure Library module on **Computer Operations Management**.*

In their respective subject areas, the IT Infrastructure Library publications complement and provide more detail than the IS Guides.

The ethos behind the development of the IT Infrastructure Library is the recognition that organizations are becoming increasingly dependent on IT in order to satisfy their corporate aims and meet their business needs. This growing dependency leads to a growing requirement for high-quality IT services. In this context quality means matched to business needs and user requirements as these evolve.

This module is one of a series of codes of practice intended to facilitate the quality management of IT Services, and of the IT Infrastructure. (By IT Infrastructure, we mean organizations' computers and networks - hardware, software and computer-related telecommunications, upon which applications systems and IT services are built and run). The codes of practice are intended to assist organizations to provide quality IT service in the face of skill shortages, system complexity, rapid change, current and future user requirements, growing user expectations, etc.

Underpinning the IT Infrastructure is the Environmental Infrastructure upon which it is built. Environmental topics are covered in a separate set of guides within the IT Infrastructure Library.

IT Infrastructure Management is a complex subject which for presentational and practical reasons has been broken down within the IT Infrastructure Library into a series of modules. A complete list of current and planned modules is available from the CCTA IT Infrastructure Management Services at the address given at the back of this module.

The structure of this module is in essence :

* *a Management summary aimed at senior IT managers (Directors of IT and above) and some "senior customers"; (typically Civil Service grades 3 - 7)*

* *the main body of the text aimed at IT middle management (typically grades 7 to HEO).*

*The module gives the main **guidance** in sections 3 to 5; explains the **benefits, costs and possible problems** in section 6, which may be of interest to senior staff; and provides information on **tools** (requirements and examples of real-life availability) in section 7.*

CCTA is working with the IT industry to foster the development of software tools to underpin the guidance contained within the codes of practice (ie to make adherence to the module more practicable), and ultimately to automate functions.

If you have any comments on this or other modules, do please let us know. A comment sheet is provided with every module; please feel free to photocopy the comment sheet or to let us have your views via any other medium.

Thank you. We hope you find this module useful.

Section 1
Management summary

1. Management summary

This module is intended to help Computer Operations Managers organize and run their computer operations to provide quality IT services to satisfy their organization's business needs.

Background

Many organizations have a computer operations function which has been in existence for a long time. However, changes in the way IT is used, including the trend towards online systems and the dispersal of computing away from the centre, are changing the responsibilities of the computer operations function. For example, a computer operations function must accommodate the following trends in IT service provision:

* IT services are becoming subject to unpredictable demand and are being increasingly perceived as utilities like water and electricity; to satisfy business needs these services must be of good quality and users expect this

* batch processing is being relegated to overnight slots which are often tightly timed and must finish in time to allow the resumption of the online day service

* increasingly the level of IT service provided to customers is formalized in Service Level Agreements (SLAs).

To cope with the changing responsibilities of the computer operations function and to exploit technological advances and an increase in automation, computer operations practices are changing, with for example:

* the introduction of Operations Bridges which collocate the computer operations and network control staff, and the Help Desk

* the 'lights-out' and unattended operation of equipment

* the trend towards operations analysts rather than operators.

Against this background of change, computer operations management has other problems to contend with - notably the difficulty of engaging and retaining suitably skilled staff, containing costs, and keeping abreast of technological change.

The IT Infrastructure Library
Computer Operations Management

This module

This module gives guidance to organizations' computer operations functions on the practices they must follow to ensure that quality services (eg as specified in SLAs) can be provided.

The guidance in the module can be applied by organizations irrespective of how far they have got in modernising their practices and procedures.

The module helps computer operations management to solve the problems of skill shortages, cost pressures and rapid technological change by giving a structured approach to computer operations management. Together with the other modules in the IT Infrastructure Library, this module provides a coherent approach to the cost-effective provision of quality IT services.

2. Introduction

Note — In this module the term Computer Operations is abbreviated to Ops as this is accepted terminology throughout the industry.

2.1 Purpose

The purpose of this module is to give guidance to organizations' IT management on how to plan and manage the operation of their computer facilities to meet their requirements for quality IT services. The module covers all aspects of the day-to-day running of an Ops function and includes guidance on the planning, implementation and review of the function.

2.2 Target readership

IT Services Managers; Ops Managers and their staff.

2.3 Scope

This module defines procedures for the operation of computer hardware and software (including remote distributed systems) to provide scheduled services. Coverage includes details of:

* Ops' role in providing a quality service
* operability standards
* interfaces to other IT infrastructure management disciplines and to applications development
* state of the art in Ops.

The guidance stresses the need to define the limit of the Ops function's responsibility and delegated freedom (eg the rules under which it can withdraw the service need to be strictly defined and adhered to).

The guidance covers the move towards greater Ops productivity, making use of the Operations Bridge, and the advance in automating Ops. It also covers the trend towards operations analysts and the implications of that trend.

The module does not cover:

* unattended operating or network management, in any detail
* hardware maintenance (including third party and single source maintenance)

* the planning and management of hardware installation and implementation.

There are separate modules on each of these subjects.

2.4 Related guidance

This book is one of a series of modules issued as part of the CCTA IT Infrastructure Library. Although this module can be read in isolation, it should be used in conjunction with other IT Infrastructure Library modules. The following modules are most relevant.

Service Level Management

Ops management and service level management are complementary activities. The nature of the IT service to be provided by Ops, and the resources needed to do it, are determined by the contents of Service Level Agreements. (SLAs). The way in which SLAs must be managed is described in the Service Level Management module. The satisfactory achievement of agreed service levels depends on the quality of computer operations as described in this module.

Computer Installation & Acceptance

A number of activities which are often the responsibility of Ops are described in the Computer Installation and Acceptance module. These include management of site planning, preparation of computer accommodation, supervision of vendors during installation, acceptance testing, parallel running and management of some forms of in-situ upgrades.

Unattended Operating

A separate module is available on unattended operating. Organizations that intend running a mixture of attended/unattended, or totally unattended, are advised to refer to that module.

Change Management

The Change Management module gives guidance on how to manage changes to IT services and procedures. The controlled implementation of change is essential to minimize risk to IT services. Changes to Ops procedures must be subject to the change management process.

Section 2
Introduction

Configuration Management

The release of configuration items into the Ops environment must be controlled and recorded. The Configuration Management module gives guidance on how best to do that. Ops may be responsible for checking the authorization status of hardware and software items to be installed on the IT infrastructure or to be released into live use.

The Configuration Management module covers:

* identification and recording of hardware and software items on the IT infrastructure

* control of changes to the IT infrastructure

* audit of the IT infrastructure to check that it contains all, and only, authorized items.

Help Desk

The Help Desk module explains how to set up and run a Help Desk to deal with user enquiries. The Help Desk and Ops work closely together to handle IT service incidents, ideally using a common system to record and progress incidents. Increasingly the Help Desk and Ops are collocated on an Ops Bridge to improve and speed up communications.

Problem Management

The Problem Management module gives advice on the handling of incidents and problems including those that affect, and those that are handled by, Ops.

Network Management

The Network Management module gives guidance on the management and operation of telecommunications equipment. Procedures for the operation of computer and telecommunications equipment should be complementary. Often both functions are housed together on an Ops Bridge to improve human communications.

Availability Management

Ops is normally responsible for ensuring that the contracted maintenance of equipment is carried out to sustain the availability of IT services and for managing recovery after failures. The Availability Management module covers the planning and management of IT infrastructures and systems to help ensure they meet reliability and availability requirements.

Contingency Planning

Plans to recover the IT service in the event of a disaster normally impact heavily on Ops. The Contingency Planning module gives guidance on the plans required.

Vendor Management

Ops often have day to day working relationships with vendors of IT equipment and services. Advice on how these relationships should be conducted is contained in the Vendor Management module.

Customer Liaison

Operability standards need to be formulated and agreed with users. The behaviour of Ops can affect users and vice versa. Regular reviews should take place and any necessary corrective action should be instigated. The Customer Liaison module covers these issues.

Software Control & Distribution

Ops can be made responsible for ensuring that only authorized software releases are used to provide live service. The Software Control and Distribution module covers the release and implementation of software for live use.

Capacity Management

Ops may be given devolved responsibility for monitoring system performance, reporting on exceptions/problems to the Capacity Management team, and for day to day tuning activities under the overall control of Capacity Management. The Capacity Management module includes guidance on performance monitoring and system tuning.

Section 2
Introduction

2.5 Standards

BS6650 Code of practice for the control of the operation of a computer.

This standard makes recommendations for the control of the operation of a computer (or computers). The standard covers the:

* hardware
* computer environment and the equipment used to control the environment
* protection of programs
* input data
* output data and the media on which that data is stored while it is the responsibility of those who operate the computer.

ISO 9000 series, EN29000 and BS5750 - quality management and quality assurance standards

The IT Infrastructure Library codes of practice are being designed to assist their adherents to obtain third-party quality certification to ISO 9001. Organizations' IT Directorates may wish to be so certified and CCTA may in future recommend that Facilities Management providers are also certified.

The IT Infrastructure Library
Computer Operations Management

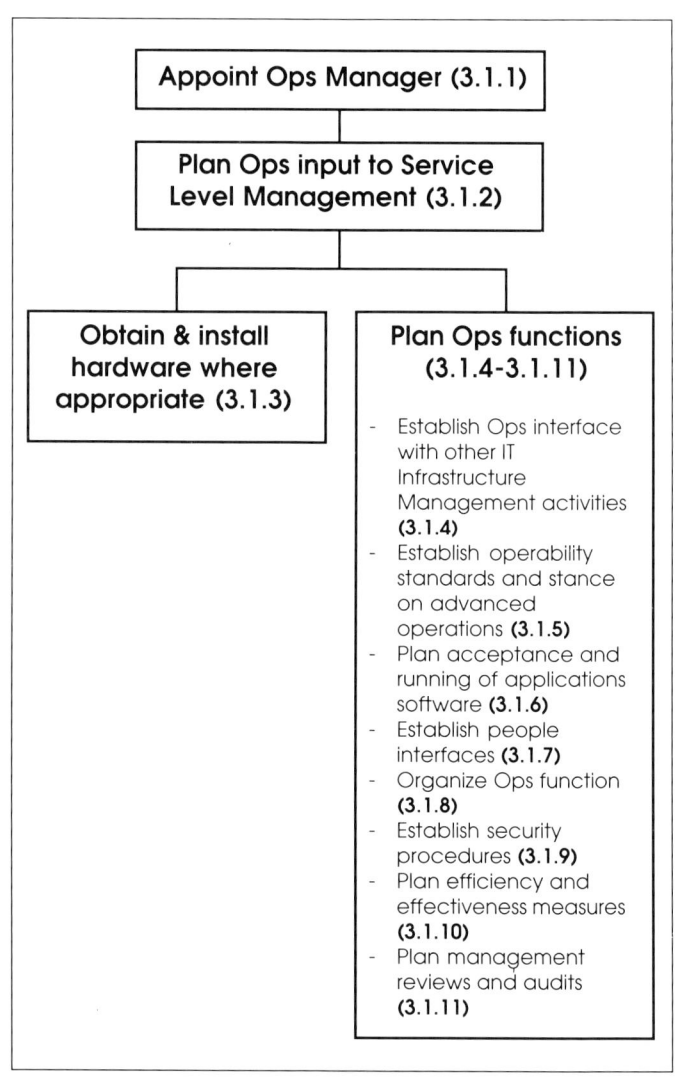

Figure 1: Diagrammatic representation of when to do & where to find guidance in 3.1

3. Planning for computer operations management

This section gives guidance on the planning of an Ops Management function.

All the processes described are required for an effective Ops organization, but there are likely to be local variations dependent on staffing levels, hardware and software in use, and business requirements.

The processes are valid in both 'greenfield' and established sites.

In all cases new processes should be introduced using a project management method, preferably PRINCE. Further guidance on project management is contained in CCTA IS Guide A5 - Project Managers' Guide - published by Wileys.

Throughout this module the keynote is that Ops must provide an efficient and cost-effective service to the business. All the processes are designed to bring that about.

3.1 Procedures

Figure 1, opposite, is a diagrammatic representation of the structure of section 3.1; this figure shows the main activities involved in planning an Ops function, and the sequence in which they should be carried out.

Out of the activities covered in 3.1 comes a set of ongoing Ops procedures. These should be documented in an Ops manual.

3.1.1 The Operations Manager

The IT Services Manager should arrange for someone to be appointed as Ops Manager if the post is not already filled. It is crucial that the Ops Manager is given the correct scope. The Ops Manager's role has to be defined clearly, not only for the person concerned but also for his/her peers, subordinates and superiors. The most effective way to define this role is to scope it in a 'mission (target) statement', which should be developed with the appointee. The job objectives that are then developed must support the mission. Mission, objectives and targets should be included in the Ops Manager's job description. Annex B contains an example mission statement and job description.

3.1.1.1 Experience

The appointee needs to be capable of achieving the mission and the objectives and targets. The qualities and areas of experience needed are:

* Ops experience, preferably in an installation with the same scale of operation as that being planned, and across the whole area of machine room, data control, scheduling, etc - normally a minimum of 2 years in a senior supervisory position, eg as a shift leader, is recommended

* experience of the hardware and software environment to be utilized - although general management and business skills are more important than having worked with the particular hardware and software concerned

* management ability - direct line-management skills are required

* business appreciation - an understanding of the business targets of the operation is essential to appreciate the true criticality of the Ops role

* an appreciation of the concepts of service level management (see the IT Infrastructure Library module on **Service Level Management**) - experience of having been a user could be beneficial

* a general understanding of the technical and business issues associated with IT, and ideally experience of working in a non-Ops area such as application development

* financial management - the position-holder often has a large budget to administer, and skills in this area are important (see the IT Infrastructure Library module on **Cost Management**)

* project management skills - many Ops tasks should be run as development/implementation projects to ensure deliverables are produced to quality and on time (PRINCE is the CCTA recommended method for project management)

* adaptability to change - essential as the IT environment is constantly changing in terms both of the way it works and of what it uses (see also the IT Infrastructure Library module on **Change Management**)

Section 3
Planning for computer operations management

* an understanding of the principles of IT infrastructure management as described in the IT Infrastructure Library.

3.1.1.2 When to appoint the Ops Manager

Established site

In an established site, appointment of the Ops Manager normally takes place prior to the departure of the existing manager. If this is not possible, the most suitable internal candidate should be given the responsibility on a temporary basis until a permanent appointment can be made.

Greenfield site

In a greenfield situation the position must be filled prior to the actual installation of the equipment to allow the Ops Manager to contribute to that process and to allow time, for example, to:

* recruit and train a team
* set up procedures as described in this module
* develop working arrangements with other managers.

The optimum time to appoint the Ops Manager is some time between the signing of the hardware procurement contracts and 3-6 months before installation of the hardware, giving a defined lead-time and also early contact with vendors. This itself may well be 6-12 months before service provision commences. Remember to include lead time for advertising, interviewing and appointing which is likely to be approximately 3 months.

Other influencing factors are whether the Ops Manager is needed to provide input to the processes of setting up a computer room, acquiring the system software and deciding the hardware configuration - perhaps necessitating an earlier appointment.

The final decision on when to appoint the Ops Manager depends on achieving a balance between the costs of early appointment and the risks of having too much to achieve if the appointment is later - invariably earlier is better.

3.1.1.3 How to grade the post

For Government organizations, grading of posts within the IT Functional Specialism is primarily determined against the criteria for grades in the Administrative Group. Grading within Government organizations is the responsibility of Personnel Management Groups. However, organizations may find the following generic guidance useful.

Factors that should be considered before deciding on grade and salary issues are:

* number of staff being supervised
* local pay scales/gradings
* industry skill shortages
* job criticality (how critical are the IT services to the business and how important are they likely to become; how critical is the role of Ops to the provision of IT services)
* the level of budget to be managed
* equivalent grade/pay levels in other installations (within Government and outside)
* the flexibility needed to attract staff who are to be recruited
* the grade and salary of other managers in the installation.

In essence the grade must reflect the job mission and objectives. Section 3.3.1 contains further advice on possible job comparisons for staff in Ops.

3.1.2 Service Level Requirements

For new or existing systems the meeting of Service Level Requirements is the *raison d'être* of IT Services. Ops should be asked to contribute to decision-making on:

* SLRs
* the hardware to buy to support the SLRs
* scheduling of workloads
* how to measure adherence to SLAs.

Ops must clearly understand "we're in business to adhere to SLAs".

Ops must participate in the planning of the IT infrastructure management processes required to ensure that SLAs are adhered to. Ops must ensure that their contribution to the meeting of SLAs is maintained, or improved upon, throughout the life of computer equipment and systems.

Section 3
Planning for computer operations management

3.1.3 Computer installation and acceptance

This section gives an overview of Ops' responsibility for the installation and acceptance of computer systems. These activities are covered in greater detail in the IT Infrastructure Library module on **Computer Installation and Acceptance**.

3.1.3.1 Installation

Computer installation and acceptance should be run as a formal project, preferably using PRINCE. The Project Manager, who is probably the Ops Manager or Ops Manager designate, must plan to ensure that:

* power, air-conditioning and other environmental supplies are performing to specification before installation of hardware

* when hardware is delivered, it goes through the configuration management process before coming under Ops' control

* the hardware is installed by the engineers in accordance with the conditions of the contract, typically

    - the hardware is as ordered and in good condition (ie with no physical damage or paint defects)

    - any special features requested are supplied

    - the hardware is installed at the time specified and installation does not take longer than specified

    - the hardware is installed at the specified location within the organization's building

    - fallback/regression arrangements if installation is not successful, are as specified

* installation conforms in a physical sense to the necessary computer room layout with working clearances around devices as specified and to air conditioning/power constraints - this layout will normally have been documented in an installation plan developed with Ops' involvement.

3.1.3.2 Commissioning

Once the equipment is installed, the Ops Manager must plan to work closely with the vendor to ensure that commissioning of the equipment is carried out in the minimum possible time. To this end, regular liaison meetings should be held to check the progress against the contract specification.

The Ops Manager must ensure that Ops staff remain in close contact with vendor staff, to keep abreast of any possible problem situations and to check that diagnostic routines have been thoroughly carried out by the vendor engineers. This close working relationship should ease the task of getting the equipment operational as quickly as possible. It is probably the Ops Manager who has to recommend during this time if any fallback/regression arrangements must be invoked.

3.1.3.3 Acceptance testing

Once equipment is operational, Ops must plan to run a suite of programs of known functionality and performance to check that the system runs as expected. If equipment is procured under CCTA's CC88 rules, then once commissioning is complete, an acceptance trial is required. The type of trial will be specified in the procurement contract. The usual acceptance procedure is that contained in Part 3-A of CC88, requiring certain levels of serviceability to be met over a specified period whilst running a workload. The workload should be similar to that described in the OR or as otherwise specified in the contract. If further demonstrations of performance or functionality are required, these should also be specified in the contract. Ops must plan to monitor the conduct of the trial and run any contractually specified demonstrations. The equipment must be accepted only following successful completion of these tests.

If equipment is new to the Ops section, staff must be trained in its operation - training may be included in the cost of the contract. If the organization's staff are to run the equipment while it is being tested, they must be trained before the trials begin.

Section 3
Planning for computer operations management

3.1.4 Operations interface with other IT infrastructure management activities

Ops is an integral part of IT infrastructure management. It is important that Ops should plan to work closely with other IT infrastructure management functions to ensure that its role is fully effective.

3.1.4.1 Problem management interface

Ops shares responsibility, with other IT infrastructure management groups, for incident control. Incident control is the part of problem management that is concerned with restoring normal service operation as quickly as possible with minimal impact on the user community. A common set of procedures should be used by all functions responsible for incident control.

Ops' responsibilities for incident control comprise the following activities for incidents that occur in the Ops domain; ie for those incidents that affect the normal operation of the IT equipment that is under Ops' control (network control and the Help Desk deal with incidents occurring in the network and user domains respectively):

* recording incidents - on forms or screens (and ensuring that contractual documentation is complete)
* alerting other control staff (Network Control and Help Desk) that an incident has occurred
* identifying the reason for the incident, where possible, and hence the appropriate resolution action, eg calling in a hardware engineer
* calling for assistance from Problem Management when Ops is unable to identify the reason
* recovering and restoring the IT service according to pre-defined procedures
* notifying the Help Desk when the incident is closed and when the service is fully restored.

A problem management support tool, common to Ops, Help Desk, network management and problem management/specialist support staff is normally used to facilitate a common approach, across these functions, to incident control.

Ops must participate in the review of all incidents affecting it. For any incident that does not have symptoms that match those of a known problem, a new problem record must be raised to indicate that the root cause is unknown. Once the root cause is known the problem is converted to a known error. The root cause could be a variety of things including, for example, mis-operations or faulty equipment.

Ops must participate in the review of problems and known errors affecting it. The purpose of Ops' participation in these reviews is to ensure that Ops:

* helps to resolve its 'own' problems

* contributes to the resolution of cross-function problems

* puts right any deficiencies in its own procedures, staff training, purchasing, or contracts.

3.1.4.2 Configuration and change management interface

Configuration management is concerned with:

* identifying and recording all items (hardware, software and telecommunications equipment) in an IT infrastructure

* controlling all changes to the IT infrastructure (change management can be regarded as a subset of configuration management)

* periodically auditing the IT infrastructure to check that it contains only authorized items.

All changes to the IT infrastructure, including the delivery or installation of new hardware and software, must be done under the control of configuration management. The state of the IT infrastructure at any time, and details of any changes authorized to it, must be recorded in the configuration management database. Ops is responsible for ensuring that no equipment deliveries or changes take place without configuration management authorization and for ensuring that only authorized software is loaded and run by the operators.

Section 3
Planning for computer operations management

Change management is designed to allow the logical and orderly planning and implementation of changes to:

* any component of the IT infrastructure or of the IT services

* procedures affecting the delivery of the IT services.

Ops contributes input in the form of changes that it wishes to make, to add to or change any item of IT service, system hardware, software or the environment, or to change any procedures that directly affect people outside Ops. The Ops Manager must ensure that Ops changes are notified to Change Management and considered in the correct timeframe. Ops should participate in the change scheduling and review process, to ensure that the operation of equipment, upon which the successful delivery of the service is dependent, is not adversely affected.

3.1.4.3 Network management interface

As the network provides the means for the IT services to reach the users, it needs to be managed in close harmony with Ops, and the dividing line of responsibility needs to be drawn. This dividing line is usually at the Front End Processors(FEPs), with the Network Manager being responsible for all the configuration outboard of the FEPs. Ops is responsible for the equipment inboard, including sometimes the FEP. The Ops Bridge management and control centre is a common vehicle for managing the computer system and network in unison. See 3.2.3.1 for more information on Bridge operations. Computer Ops and network/network management changes must **always** be notified to the other area through the change management process.

3.1.4.4 Cost management interface

Ops may have allocated to its budget the capital cost of equipment, and the running costs of hardware, accommodation and environment. In any event, the Ops function has significant staffing costs. Effective budgetary controls must exist and the Ops Manager must collaborate with the IT Cost Manager to set these up. The Ops Manager must be able to provide the IT Cost Manager with detailed cost breakdowns for both forecast and actual figures at the appropriate accounting intervals. The Ops Manager must conduct regular cost control reviews to help ensure that Ops operates efficiently and cost-effectively.

The IT Infrastructure Library
Computer Operations Management

3.1.4.5 Contingency planning interface

Ops must have input to the installation's contingency plan. It has to help establish the facilities that would be required in the event of a disaster or a severe degradation of IT services. The basic need is to run the identified critical applications within the disaster recovery timeframe indicated. The contingency plan and hence the Ops element of it, should be tested at least once a year.

3.1.4.6 Help Desk interface

The Help Desk provides first level support to all users of the IT services. Ops is required to liaise closely with the Help Desk, to communicate Ops incidents and one-off service changes that are likely to affect user services, to gain information on user priorities at different time periods, and to respond quickly to users' difficulties and queries. See also 3.1.7.1.

3.1.4.7 Operations role

All the topics described above are covered in depth in separate IT Infrastructure Library modules. The key points are that Ops has an important role in supporting many IT Directorate functions and Ops must adhere to procedures defined by these functions. IT services cannot be delivered without Ops. In many smaller organizations some of the functions listed may well be Ops' responsibilities. Individuals within Ops may be responsible for more than one function.

In every case Ops should ensure that it uses the procedures described in other IT Infrastructure Library modules positively, as tools to help it in its role - they are all aids to an effective IT organization and they can help organizations set and maintain the standards of IT service required. Active cooperation with respect to procedures that are not run by Ops is essential - liaise with the relevant manager to assess how to contribute.

3.1.4.8 Operations Support Group

In many medium to large organizations a distinction is nowadays made between the Ops shift staff and 'office hours' Operations Support Group(OSG). The shift function can be seen as the production line providing the end service, in terms of running batch and online systems, while OSG provide and maintain standards, documentation, Ops

Section 3
Planning for computer operations management

tools; and the interface with the rest of IT infrastructure management. In this module, the term operator refers to shift Ops personnel and the term operations analyst refers to a member of the OSG team.

The formation of the OSG function provides an opportunity for talented operators to develop their potential within Ops instead of automatically moving outside the Ops domain for career progression. The shift environment has become the proving ground for operations analysts.

3.1.5 Operability standards and the move to advanced Ops

3.1.5.1 Operability standards

Operability standards must be defined for software developed in-house to ensure that the requirement of Ops for efficient operations is satisfied. Ops should involve Application Development Managers in the defining of operability standards. Within Ops, the task of defining these standards would normally be driven by the operations analysts.

Typically, operability standards cover the items described below.

Efficient design

Organizations should have standards that encourage the best design of applications to make the most efficient and effective use of the available IT systems. These standards should be defined in collaboration with the Capacity Manager.

Security

Standards to protect applications software and data from malevolent access and tampering should be defined in collaboration with the IT Security Manager.

Minimization of operator console intervention

Operators should not have to respond continually to 'pause' messages on the console. Programs should not send messages to the operators' console at all. Operators should not be expected to input runtime parameters or amend JCL listings.

Limiting the use of special stationery and the number of paper changes

The use of generic forms for application suites should be encouraged to minimize the number of forms used and save on printing costs. The use of paper-drum, laser or remote-user-location printing limits the paper change interventions required.

The IT Infrastructure Library
Computer Operations Management

Limiting tape mounts — Tapes (with the exception of automatically-loaded cartridge tapes) are a relatively inefficient and slow form of data input and storage. Their use should be reserved for essential housekeeping (backups, etc) and transfers to other sites, microfiche and the like.

Effective use of disk space — Standards should be set in collaboration with the organization's Capacity Manager, or Magnetic Storage Manager, for the use of disk space by all applications. The aim is to use space efficiently and to optimize run-time efficiency.

Recovery and rerun routines — Applications should be recoverable quickly, simply, and where possible automatically. For example, the need to rerun whole applications to recreate prints should be avoided. Recovery after failure should be possible in short, specified timeframes - perhaps going back only one or two program steps to recover. Long and difficult-to-segment processing steps should be avoided. Clear documentation for operators, showing the appropriate recovery and rerun actions, is vital and must be insisted upon, but automation of reruns is better. Proof should be sought that recovery and rerun has been tested.

Operator documentation — Documentation should be provided which shows the functionality, dependencies, and file layouts/relationships for application suites. This documentation is necessary both to give operators background on the applications they are running, and also to make easier the scheduling, running and recovery processes (where these are not automated).

Naming conventions — Naming conventions should be applied to items (eg filenames, job names, accounts) and structured to make the names meaningful.

3.1.5.2 Advanced operations

Advanced operations is the term used to describe an operations function in which the advances in hardware and software have been utilized to allow more automated control and where Ops personnel are taking on the more technical role of operations analysts. The term advanced operations also encompasses the reorientation of Ops staff towards a service culture based on the need to provide quality customer services.

The Ops role is becoming more skilled. Operators are taking on the role of operations analysts and assuming responsibilities within other IT infrastructure management disciplines. The labour intensive jobs are being greatly reduced, with, for example, user departments in charge of

Section 3
Planning for computer operations management

their own input and output, and an increasing use of software products to automate Ops functions. Operators need training on a wider range of skills than in the past and career paths need to be redefined and agreed.

To support a move to advanced operations, improved operability standards must be defined and planned. Automated or unattended operating require that these standards are applied particularly in the applications development area. Ops has always insisted upon high standards from suppliers of hardware and system software - similar standards are needed from internal and external suppliers of applications software and are starting to be demanded by Ops. The goal is to have applications software that facilitates:

* easier and more automatic Ops
* more efficient operation and use of systems.

3.1.5.3 Automated and unattended operating

Automated operating

Automated operating aims to automate the role of operators as far as possible. Typically automated operating features the following:

* pre-programmed replies to standard console messages
* suppression of non-critical messages
* generation of alerts to specified locations which warn of impending or actual hardware and software incidents
* routing of messages to any designated console
* minimization of the need to intervene to load, operate and unload hardware
* automation of time-critical tasks such as Initial Program Load(IPL), online systems startup and closedown
* implementation of an automated scheduling system
* implementation of a tape/disk management system
* implementation of robot devices; eg tape/cartridge loaders.

Automation greatly reduces the amount of routine activity involved in computer operations.

The IT Infrastructure Library
Computer Operations Management

More detail on the software tools that can be used to implement these features is contained in section 7. The evaluation and implementation of automated operating software is normally carried out by OSG with input from the shift operators, especially concerning areas such as message suppression and alert generation.

Unattended operating

The term unattended operating refers to the running of computers automatically without operators being present. Unattended operating may not be the goal of an organization for various practical and/or political reasons. Automated operating is valid in its own right. If unattended operating is the goal then achieving automated operating is a prerequisite to which must be added the remote and/or automated monitoring and control of the computer system itself, plus its physical environment.

The operability standards (see 3.1.5.1) are particularly necessary to enable organizations to automate operations - console activity and tape/disk and paper handling must be kept to a minimum. The quality of applications has to be good enough to allow them to run unattended if required. Ops should pay particular attention to the areas of reliability, recoverability, documentation, and console messaging in the setting of standards for automated and unattended running.

More information on these subjects is contained in the IT Infrastructure Library module on **Unattended Operating**.

3.1.6 Accepting and running applications software

To help ensure that applications software is of sufficiently good quality that it runs in live use satisfactorily, and in particular that it does not impede the smooth operation of organizations' computer systems, procedures must be defined for the acceptance and running of applications software. Ops must be involved in defining these procedures.

A plan for the Ops acceptance process should be devised. Ops needs to review new applications, as part of change management testing, and judge them against the operability standards, particularly those aspects that affect Ops. In circumstances where standards have been consistently ignored, Ops would be justified in rejecting applications, or at least demanding considerable remedial work.

Section 3
Planning for computer operations management

3.1.6.1 Applications acceptance stages

There are five acceptance stages, each of which requires an element of planning by Ops. Ops and other parts of the IT Services section are involved at each stage. This module covers only Ops' responsibilities.

Stage 1 — Ops should be involved from the earliest stages of the development to help prevent problems later. The Ops representative should typically be an operations analyst, who advises the development team of relevant operability criteria that should be applied.

Stage 2 — For the duration of the development project, the operations analyst attends project review meetings to stay abreast of the development and reports back to the Ops Manager if problems are being encountered in meeting operability criteria, and advises the project on what to do.

Stage 3 — During acceptance tests, the operations analyst should be involved in monitoring the running and operational performance of the application.

Acceptance testing should be run in a test environment set up to simulate the live environment - this separate environment avoids damage to live work.

The operations analyst, in collaboration with other IT Services staff, monitors the testing closely, recording details against the operability criteria described in 3.1.5. Any discrepancies should be highlighted for action at the post acceptance-test review with the development team. Not until the application has satisfactorily met all the criteria should it go live.

Stage 4 — When the application has been approved as ready to go live, application programs and any associated job control programs should be copied from the Definitive Software Library to the live environment(s) by the configuration management team.

All operators should be trained in the new application at this stage by the project team. (In the case of small changes the training could be limited just to the shift leaders, who would then be responsible for passing the information on to their shift team members.)

Stage 5 — Immediately prior to the application going live, the IT Services section including Ops should hold a pre-live review meeting with the development team to check the last minute details of scheduling, file dependencies, and any outstanding problems, errors and queries. There should be onsite support from the development team in case of any problems, particularly if the application is critical to the business or is on the critical processing path.

For further information on the control of software that passes into the live environment (including the use of test and live environments and of the Definitive Software Library), please refer to the IT Infrastructure Library module on **Software Control and Distribution**.

3.1.6.2 Maintaining project team links

During application development, close links must be maintained with the project team, as shown at the various stages of the application lifecycle described above, to ensure that Ops does not have to run an application that is below standard, too costly to run or support, or provides poor service to users. The application development project also benefits from Ops having a good understanding of the IT service the developers require of Ops during the development stage.

It is recommended that operations analysts are assigned to applications from early development stages to well into production - this association gives Ops and other parts of the IT Services section easy access to a knowledge base that is invaluable in case of difficulties. To guard against the loss of this knowledge, operations analysts should document their work in detail.

The operations analyst should regularly consult the shift staff during the above stages and not simply agree to procedures and systems based on past personal experience when working in the shift environment.

3.1.6.3 Ensuring the production quality of applications

It is important that the Ops Manager should not accept poor applications. Applications may take many man-years of development, but in most cases they spend much more time in production. It is in everyone's long-term interest to ensure that quality applications are implemented. More information is available in the IT Infrastructure Library modules on **Application Life-Cycle Support** and **Testing Software for Operational Use**.

Section 3
Planning for computer operations management

Ops staff must be encouraged to report difficulties they experience with software that is in live use to the problem management system, so that action can be taken to eliminate the more serious deficiencies at source and gradually improve the quality of the operational environment.

3.1.7 Operations and the people interface

Ops has historically been the IT unit that has been 'shut away' and had little exposure to:

* users

* management (unless a problem arose!)

* the business needs.

The Ops situation has changed radically with the general increase in business dependency on IT and the development of online systems.

Ops is now in the forefront of IT, and has an increasingly important role to play in the furtherance of business goals. See also 3.1.4, which explains how Ops fits into the overall management of IT.

The change in the role of Ops has led to Ops staff and managers needing to develop highly-tuned interpersonal skills to augment their technical ability. Close relationships need to be developed with the following groups of people.

3.1.7.1 The Help Desk

The Help Desk is responsible for all day-to-day contact between IT Services and its users. Ops must develop its relationship with the Help Desk by frequent (probably daily) liaison meetings. Ops should use information, gathered by Help Desk, as a barometer for the quality of the service being provided. The Help Desk provides feedback on user (and sometimes management) satisfaction with the offered service. A weekly (at least) formal meeting with the Help Desk is essential to share views on the week's service delivery and decide ways of improving the IT service. This meeting should take place in the form of a service review, and be attended by other managers key to the provision of IT services (eg Service Level Manager, Problem Manager, Change Manager, Network Manager). The meeting should be chaired by the IT Services Manager. At subsequent meetings a check should be made that follow-up actions identified in previous meetings have been successfully carried out. See also 3.1.4.6.

3.1.7.2 Users

In installations where Help Desks are not yet in place or work only daytime hours, Ops staff often represent the IT Directorate when users call in with problems or queries. It is imperative that a professional and credible image is presented to these callers. Calls need to be handled promptly and effectively. Training in interpersonal and telephone skills is essential in these installations. If, exceptionally, an organization is not planning to use a Help Desk (positively not recommended), Ops staff need to be trained in Help Desk techniques and processes. For further information please refer to the IT Infrastructure Library module on the **Help Desk**.

3.1.7.3 Technical and application support units

Ops is dependent on other units to support the system and application software. Formal liaison between the Ops Manager and the heads of these units on at least a weekly basis is needed.

Figure 2: Contact List / escalation thresholds

CONTACT LIST STOCK A/C BATCH				
Contact level escalation threshold	Name	Support Title	Phone Number	Bleep
1 (if not resolved after 5 mins)	Problem Mgt. Duty Officer	See Rota for details		
2 (after 30 mins)	R.Jones	Applic's Support	2010 (home: 0732-1111)	5077
3 (after 1 hour)	F.Roberts	Applic's Support Manager	2200 (home: 110-7542)	-
4 (after 2 hours)	L.Washton	IT Services Manager	1111 (home: 0732-4785)	-

In terms of providing day-to-day support to the running systems, Ops needs to establish reliable contact points for both daytime and out-of-hours support. The problem management section is normally responsible for resolving or escalating incidents once it has received them. However, the problem management section may pass responsibility to Ops for resolution or escalation of incidents and hardware failures in the Ops domain and of all incidents during out-of-hours working. Figure 2 shows a typical support contact list/escalation threshold for significant incidents affecting an application package.

The use of computer terminals at home is now quite common amongst support staff and should be encouraged subject to satisfactory arrangements to safeguard security, as it speeds incident resolution and provides for more productive Ops as a result.

The level of support must be sufficient to ensure that SLAs can be met.

3.1.7.4 Suppliers of hardware and services

Ops depends upon regular suppliers to provide services, and the relationship between Ops and these suppliers must be managed. The suppliers are being paid to provide a service and/or equipment in a relationship tied by contractual conditions. A very effective way to manage suppliers is to tie them in to your management disciplines. For example, with respect to problem management, if there are system software 'bugs' outstanding with your vendor, there should be a response in the timeframe specified. If not, the same escalation processes that are used for internal problems should be applied. The vendor's Account Manager should be used to instigate management action from the vendor company when the agreed thresholds have been breached.

With respect to change management, if hardware vendors wish to install new or modify existing equipment or software they must be subject to the organization's normal change management system.

The management of suppliers hinges around good communications. Regular meetings with suppliers and maintainers are essential. Monitor the suppliers' and maintainers' adherence to contract and insist on corrective action in case of non-adherence. If the non-adherence is subject to contractual redress, invoke the appropriate procedures. For more information please read the IT Infrastructure Library module on **Vendor Management**.

3.1.8 Computer operations

Ops is responsible for ensuring that the online and batch processing services are run in accordance with standards and working practices agreed with IT management and suppliers. The services must normally be available during set hours and they must be run in a way that enables them to meet user requirements. Increasingly these requirements are being formalized and specified in Service Level Agreements(SLAs).

The scope of Ops' responsibilities for processing services varies from site to site in the activities performed, the shifts manned, and the periods over which service is provided.

Most of the tasks performed by Ops on a day to day basis are concerned with operating the batch service. The online service is monitored and controlled.

Figure 3 shows the typical flow of input and output data through a batch system. The phases shown in figure 3 are described in the following subsections.

3.1.8.1 Input control and the Data Control section

Increasingly, end users are inputting their own data via online systems. If this is the case, the SLAs should define who is responsible for the input data. However, some installations still have extensive batch processing facilities and sections 3.1.8.1 - 3.1.8.9 are relevant to them.

Input control, the procedures for the admission into the Ops area of all raw data, is carried out by the data control section which is part of the Ops function.

Input data standards should be agreed and documented in SLAs. These standards include the timetable for receiving and processing input and the standard layout for input data forms.

The data comes into Data Control from either internal user sections or from external sources, such as mailing companies or computer bureaux. The data may come in written form or on media such as magnetic tapes, data cartridges or diskettes.

Section 3
Planning for computer operations management

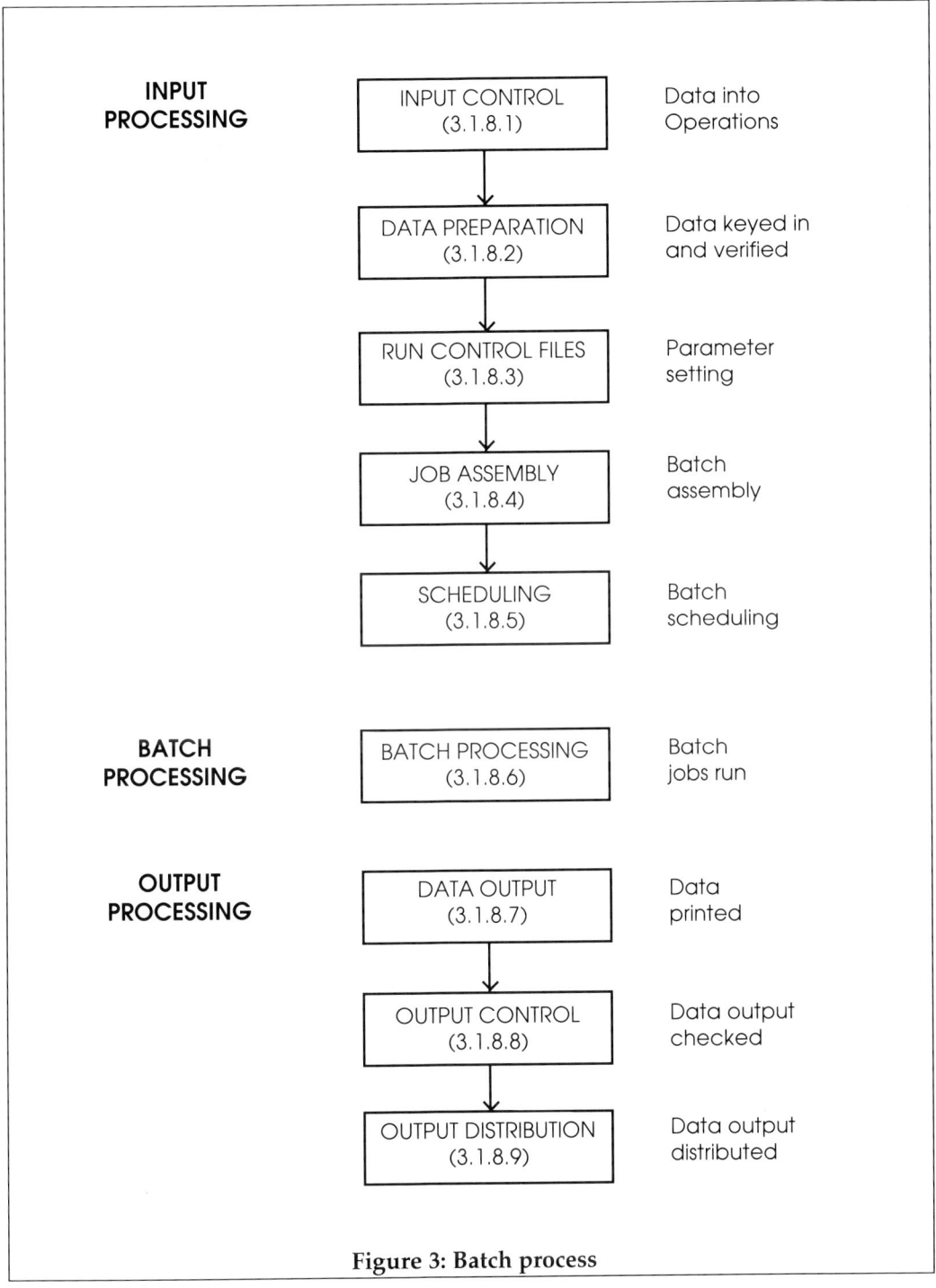

Figure 3: Batch process

The planning for the input control process should define logs and procedures. The logs are to record information:

* about the data to enable its progress to be monitored, including

    - date of receipt

    - origin of data (which section, company)

    - type of data (eg sales ledger, invoices, payments etc)

    - priority (how urgent is the job the data is for)

    - job number (assign a number to make it easy to monitor progress)

    - batch number (the input forms should be batched up for ease of processing)

* for magnetic media input

    - file layout (field lengths, etc)

    - logical record length/blocking factor

    - media density

    - number of records on media

    - printout of header.

The procedures produced must explain:

* how to use the logs provided

* what to do with each type of data - magnetic media/ written forms

    - how and to whom the data is to be passed

    - how to assign priority

    - how to deal with problems.

There also need to be deadlines for inputting data. These deadlines should be included in SLAs, as in the following example:

> "Any data for batch processing must be received by input control at or before 16:00 hours on the day of processing. Any urgent data received after 16:00 hours must be assessed by the input control supervisor, the scheduling supervisor and the shift leader. This assessment takes place only if requested by the user in charge of the data."

Section 3
Planning for computer operations management

Any input data forms not processed at the end of each day should be placed in a fireproof safe within Data Control.

3.1.8.2 Data preparation

Data preparation is the function of turning raw data into an acceptable form of input data for jobs to be run on the computer.

The data preparation function can be carried out centrally or by end users inputting their own data via online systems. For large batch environments there is often a dedicated Data Preparation section.

Whoever carries out data preparation the following procedures need to be in place:

* how to input each type of data - magnetic media/ written forms
* how to use any specific data preparation equipment
* what to do in the event of data problems (most data would be sent back to the originator)
* the procedures to be adopted in the event of an incident affecting the system being used for data preparation.

The rest of this section relates to the preparation of data by a central Data Preparation section for batch processing.

Input data, having passed through Data Control, is now ready to be keyed or, if already on magnetic media and it is necessary, converted. Inputting of data is normally done via an online system, by keying input directly to disk.

Once the data has been keyed or converted it can be verified. Verification is normally done in one or more of the following ways, depending on the nature and importance of the job and data:

* the Data Preparation section keys the data in again and the results are checked for any disparities - paper input only
* a special verification job is run, before the actual batch job, which does not update any files and therefore allows any corrections to be made before the update job is run
* the update job itself checks the data and rejects inadmissible data for processing in a subsequent run.

Once the data has been verified as correct, it is ready for processing.

Standards for input data submission should be established and used as a reference for all new applications. These standards, set up with the users and tied in with the SLAs, would include:

* expected speed of turnround of data - linked to the SLAs covering input control
* standard of input from the users, with input data that is not up to the agreed standard to be sent back to the originator.

3.1.8.3 Run Control Files

Most batch jobs have their own Run Control File (RCF) which contains parameters that may need changing before running the job.

The following examples show two uses of RCFs:

* a job containing Program A is run every month; every three months the RCF is changed to get Program A to produce extra statistics
* a job producing invoices needs a date two days before the run date to be put on the invoices; an RCF change is used.

Wherever possible it is best to dispense with RCFs or, if that is not possible, to keep them small so as to minimize the need for human intervention and reduce the opportunities for making errors.

In the first example, the RCF could be dispensed with by changing the program to run the extra tasks every third month automatically.

In the second example, a linkage to system date could be used and the earlier date achieved by specifying "system date minus 2 days".

Each RCF should have the same format if possible, to simplify maintenance. Different processors and programming languages would obviously affect the practicality of this.

RCFs would normally be set up, for jobs that require them, by the data control section but end users could set them up themselves if the rest of the input processing is done by them.

Section 3
Planning for computer operations management

The procedures should cover the following:

* for each job
    - how to access the RCF
    - how to change the parameters and what the options are
    - the RCF layout
    - what to expect from each change to the RCF
    - what to do about problems
* general
    - a schedule of what RCF changes need to be done on each day.

3.1.8.4 Job assembly

Job assembly constitutes the bringing together of the component parts of a job to be run on the computer system.

The job control, input data, parameters (RCF) and programs should be put together to make up the job or job suites to be run. When this assembly is complete, a job submission sheet should be completed.

There are packages that check job assembly before running the job. Most job failures are caused by invalid job control. As unattended and automated operations expand, the impact of, and the time wasted due to, invalid job control increases. Therefore these packages are of tremendous value.

Job assembly is normally performed by the data control section, although at smaller sites this could be done by the operators. Also, end users may set up jobs ready for submission, especially if the rest of the input process - for example data preparation - is done by them.

The procedures for job assembly should require that the following items are produced for each job or job suite:

* suite composition (ie a flow diagram of the programs that comprise the suite)
* frequency with which the job suite runs, and when

* list of jobsteps and what they do
  - eg daily: jobstep 1 validation
                  jobstep 2 update
                  jobstep 3 backup
* JCL listing (note that any JCL coding should be supplied by OSG)
* description of the parameters and what they should look like
* information on what the data should look like (eg column 1 should be a D)
* sample screen formats
  - if the job assembly is performed using an online system or
  - the application presents the operators with console messages that require response/action
* instructions on how to access job control and programs to perform permitted adjustments
* any special instructions, eg any deviations from the norm must be logged, extra copies of reports are to be printed
* instructions on how to complete the job submission sheet - if a scheduling package is used, there is no need for the job submission sheet.

3.1.8.5 Scheduling

Scheduling involves the continuous organization of jobs and processes into the most efficient sequence, maximizing throughput and utilization to meet targets set in SLAs. Jobs are scheduled to ensure:

* SLAs and user requirements are met eg certain jobs need to be run by a certain time
* available capacity is used effectively - the workload run at any given time does not exceed the practical capacity.

The overall schedule-profile of organizations' workloads - the profile of which jobs are normally run when - should therefore be decided in collaboration with the Service Level Manager and the Capacity Manager. Ops analysts are normally in charge of the scheduling day-to-day.

Section 3
Planning for computer operations management

Wherever possible, and provided that it is cost-effective, organizations should use scheduling packages that can automate most or all of the scheduling process. Such packages aim to ensure that:

* SLAs and user requirements are met
* available capacity is not exceeded.

It is recommended that in a large installation the scheduling is performed by a software package. Information about scheduling packages is given in section 7.

If a scheduling package is to be used, a formal project needs to be set up to implement it. The duration and complexity of the project should not be under-estimated. Eventually the package needs to embrace all the jobs run at the site, but a phased implementation is recommended. For instance, all jobs using the payroll files may be converted to the scheduling package first. Procedures covering the use and maintenance of the package need to be written.

Where scheduling software does not exist, the task should be done manually. At smaller sites the operators themselves could do the scheduling. The scheduling role and responsibilities must be clearly defined. In an online environment, where the whole input process has been done by the users, they could schedule their own jobs within operationally defined limits, subject to SLAs.

To define schedules, the workloads are broken down into daily, weekly, monthly and annual periods. Jobs are then timed to start according to:

* priority of the job and time its output is required - the business needs
* length of job - estimation of the elapsed time
* size of storage needed
* associated dependencies - whether the job must run before or after other jobs.

The IT Infrastructure Library
Computer Operations Management

The majority of batch jobs are run overnight or during silent hours because:

* online systems are in use during the day and batch jobs could cause problems with response times

* data input is normally done during the day

* files used by batch processing jobs are very often unavailable during the day as online users are updating them.

The scheduling procedures should cover:

* how to set up a schedule

* how to maintain the schedule

* how to deal with any problems affecting the setting up or arising from the use of schedules

* the next step in the process - pass the schedule to the operators by a set time.

Schedules need to be flexible enough to cater for ad-hoc jobs and unexpected problems. The conditions under which ad-hoc jobs are permitted to be run should be covered by SLAs. Experienced shift leaders on evening and night shift should be able to reschedule jobs, within clearly-defined limits, with the aid of the available job documentation. During the normal working day these types of changes would be handled by the normal scheduling function. Any such rescheduling should be recorded in the shift log. At all times SLAs must be adhered to.

3.1.8.6 Batch processing

Batch processing describes the phase during which jobs are run according to the work schedule, run priority, and job dependencies.

The jobs scheduled for running are released from the input queue into a batch queue and run in the correct sequence. The deadlines for all jobs are covered by SLAs.

Batch processing is performed by Ops, albeit frequently nowadays under automatic control.

Even with more sites adopting unattended/automated operations, there still need to be responsible 'experts' - operations analysts - who set up batch processing procedures to give smooth batch operations and who can

Section 3
Planning for computer operations management

iron out day-to-day problems. These experts must consider the overall needs of the business, not just the interests of one user section.

Batch processing procedures should include the following:

* job documentation - description of the documentation required for each job (see 3.2.2.2 for more details)

* instructions on how to use the hardware - eg tape units, data cartridge units, printers

* console operating - eg how to release jobs from the input queue

* message explanations; the difference between types of messages, eg information, warnings and errors, must be made clear

* problem management instructions

* a list of information needed for each type of incident

* contact lists.

Where appropriate the procedures should be based on the hardware/software suppliers' manuals - do not invent new procedures unless there is a good reason. There should be a comprehensive library of these manuals selected on advice from suppliers and service support (problem management, specialist support and OSG) staff.

Control checks are often placed in jobs for which there is a requirement to check quickly that all the data has been processed and files have been updated correctly. For example:

> does the input master file control total + today's input control total = the output master file control total?

The task of checking these totals should be under program control; if this is not practical the totals should be output for checking by the user. If, exceptionally, a check is to be carried out by Ops, details of how this is to be done, and instructions on what to do when totals do not reconcile, must be provided in the job documentation.

3.1.8.7 Data output

Data output is the phase during which output is scheduled and actually printed. The timing of data output depends on the importance of the information, but normally most output has to be printed before the start of the next day's processing.

There are packages which automate many of the processes listed below. See section 7.6 for more details.

To make sure printing happens efficiently, the same types of output should be printed consecutively. For instance:

* all multi-part paper should be printed together - this eases the problem of decollating

* special stationery (invoices etc) should also be printed consecutively if possible - this avoids wasting time with line-ups.

The SLAs cover when and where output is to be delivered. Ops must have procedures to deal with all forms of output including special procedures for handling secure items, eg cheques - see also 3.1.9. An example of the procedures that could be used for handling cheques is given in Annex E. If it is important to the customer, this type of procedure could be included in the SLA.

In most installations, the scheduling and printing of data output is done by the operators. Increasingly, however, there are separate areas within the Ops section where all the printing is performed by special print operators. In that case the print operators schedule and print all the stationery. In any case, operators in charge of printing need to check printouts regularly for unevenness and faint print.

In installations where some or all of the printout is sent via the online system to the users for printing, responsibility for the production and quality of printout and for the management of printers and stationery needs to be clear and agreed in the SLAs. For instance, who is to be responsible for missing print?

The procedures for running batch work also cover many of the procedures required for print production, but the following should be included in output procedures:

* for the general aspects of print production

    - instructions on printer operation eg how to start printers up, how to change ribbons and toner (generally covered by suppliers' manuals)

Section 3
Planning for computer operations management

- rerun procedures for wrecked or lost printout (may be partially job-specific)

* for each job or batch

  - what special stationery is needed
  - line-up procedures for printout
  - the latest time the printout is needed by, for the next part of the process or by the user section
  - the amount of printout expected by the job or batch - this information helps the operators to assess whether a problem exists, if the amount of print produced is far more or less than expected.

Line-up procedures for printout should be in a separate manual kept beside the printers, as well as in the job documentation manuals. If the procedures are kept near the printers, the operators can reference the right line-up for any printout without having to reference the individual job documentation manuals.

The procedures should include the following for each individual stationery type:

* sample stationery
* sample line-ups
* printer settings.

It is useful to consider whether certain output needs always to be printed. An example of this is output generated by the operating system such as event logs. Instead of being printed they can be spooled to tape and printed only if they are required at a later date to investigate a problem or occurrence.

3.1.8.8 Output control

The output control process checks that all output to be distributed is as specified in the job's run procedures.

Quality checks are performed together with control checks; eg checking selected figures within the printout.

The quality of the printout expected is governed by the SLAs agreed with the users. For example, when using multi-part printout the top pages must be the same quality as single-part printout; the lower pages must be readable, but do not need to be as clear as the top pages.

Output control can be carried out by the data control section, or if a special section is set up to print the documents, that section could do the checking instead. Obviously, if the users print their output, they themselves must do any necessary control and quality checks.

The procedures for output control should cover the following checks for each job and include any necessary remedial action:

* the quantity and type of stationery expected by the job

* the quality of printout expected

* control totals - an example of expected printout that highlights the figures to check.

3.1.8.9 Output distribution

Output distribution is the process of getting output to its proper destination. Output distribution is normally carried out by the data control section, although in many installations, special sections are being set up to print and distribute the documents. The output might also be sent online to the users to print in their section. The SLAs should cover distribution responsibility.

Organizations should consider the use of a print distribution package. Section 7.6 gives more details. If such a package is used, most of the distribution is automated.

Once printed output has been checked for completeness and quality, any decollation, bursting and guillotining can be performed. The printout is then distributed.

Other types of output medium eg magnetic tapes, data cartridges, diskettes, fiche, are also distributed from output control.

There are two main types of non-paper output:

* output going to external organizations or to internal sections - this output is logged and distributed in the same way as paper output

* backup media going to offsite storage.

Section 3
Planning for computer operations management

Backups should be controlled by a media management system if one is available. In any event the correct media are selected by the output distribution section and sent out as determined by the SLAs. For backups, a procedure is needed to cover the way:

* backup copies are taken
* media records are updated
* media are transported and stored offsite, and replaced by later versions.

Output distribution procedures should cover the following:

* how to use the finishing equipment - as well as decollating machines there are some that photocopy listing paper (laser printers are, however, tending to supersede both types of equipment)
* what to do in case of incidents and problems
* what to do for each job's output
* a despatch log to be completed, which should contain
    - report title, which should also include the name by which the user recognizes the report, if this is different
    - reference number
    - date and time available
    - date and time collected or delivered
    - signature of receiver or deliverer
* a log to be filled in for non-paper output, containing, where appropriate
    - tape/disk number
    - reference number
    - date and time available
    - date and time collected or delivered
    - signature of receiver or deliverer
    - where the medium (eg fiche) is to go to.

If a print distribution package is used, the procedures must cover its use.

41

3.1.8.10 Remote operation

If it is intended that the main computer site is to operate IT equipment remotely at another site, remote console hardware, software and communications need to be installed. This remote operation must be backed by procedures concerning the connection and disconnection of the links to the remote site, together with guidelines for start up and close down of the system.

The implementation of procedures and supporting infrastructure for remote Ops should be carried out by OSG in association with other technical groups such as network management.

For processing at remotely operated sites, rules must be agreed with the users about the work that can be run and the services that can be provided. For example, there must be:

* no tape or disk loading

* no input or output handling, unless done by users on a self-service basis

* no console messages that require manual action onsite

* no requirement for Ops staff to be in attendance onsite to allocate magnetic tapes or disk-space

* clear guidance to users on what to do in case of difficulties; eg all enquiries must be made to the Help Desk

* ways of dealing with system-file full conditions either automatically or remotely

* arrangements to cover the need for engineering cover onsite; eg supervision by office services or nominated user managers.

The implications of a remote site with no operations staff need to be considered carefully. The risks of fires and sabotage need to be assessed and managed. Ideally equipment should never be powered down. Monitoring systems to check system usage, and systems for error checking online need to be installed. Message management packages are also needed. These packages allow the filtering of messages, thus restricting to essentials messages that are written to the remote operators' consoles. Section 7 gives more information on tools for running remote operations.

Section 3
Planning for computer operations management

3.1.8.11 Management of magnetic media

The responsibility for the management of magnetic media may rest with Ops, with the Capacity Manager or with a Magnetic Storage Manager.

Magnetic tapes

Ideally, magnetic tapes should be used only for job backup, recovery and offsite storage. Some files, produced by batch jobs, that are used only for the duration of a job could be put on tape, but it is recommended that this should happen only if there is not enough room for them on disk.

The only input tapes that should be used are from external sources; eg another company.

There should be tape numbering standards; for example all tapes in the range 20000 - 29999 are payroll tapes.

The number of tape generations to be retained should be based on file versions - see the **Software Control and Distribution** module for further details.

Data cartridges

Data cartridges are becoming increasingly popular in computer installations in place of magnetic tapes. This popularity is mainly due to the fact that they have a faster data transfer rate, typically up to 30% faster than magnetic tapes and can also be combined with automatic loaders and robots. The devices are more reliable and, combined with the greater reliability of the data cartridges, produce up to 10 times less data errors and corruption. Data cartridges now cost less than magnetic tapes, use up less room, and are more stable, being contained within a plastic case.

The standard for tapes should be applied unchanged to data cartridges.

Disks

Nearly all the data files should be kept on disk on the IT Directorate's premises. The capacity management section or the Magnetic Storage Manager allocates disk space and ensures efficient use of the disks. Disk initialization and recovery of a whole disk are normally performed only by Ops. Action to recover individual files and/or libraries can be undertaken by the operations support, capacity management or storage management section. There must be clear procedures outlining how to do these functions, who is responsible for doing them, and when they are to be done. Guidance on the allocation and security of disks attached to PCs, terminals and departmental small computers is contained in the IT Infrastructure Library module on the **Management of Local Processors & Terminals**.

3.1.8.12 Data storage and file libraries

Providing data storage and file libraries for the users is normally the job of the Magnetic Storage Manager or the Capacity Manager, but at some smaller sites the operations section (possibly the OSG) may perform this function. The capacity management team sets the ground rules for allocating files, and is involved in the planning of filestore allocation in greenfield sites. The capacity management team also periodically reviews allocations and the relationship between file placement and disk loading. Where they are responsible for allocating file storage, the Magnetic Storage Manager or OSG must collaborate with the capacity management team to ensure that file storage allocations do not jeopardize system performance. Further guidance on file storage allocation may be found in the **Capacity Management** module of the IT Infrastructure Library.

Often the customer liaison function within the IT Services section is responsible for initial contact with users about new work and for getting answers to the questions below. See the IT Infrastructure Library module on **Customer Liaison** for further information on the role of the customer liaison function.

It is likely that procedures for allocating filestore (including instructions for the use of software tools where applicable) will be defined by the Magnetic Storage Manager or the Capacity Manager and agreed by Ops. Job control procedures and macros for filestore allocation tasks are normally specified by the Magnetic Storage Manager or the Capacity Manager. These procedures may have to be 'packaged' if they are to be used by Ops.

Ops staff should in any event ensure that the procedures cover the following points:

* what is the user's (programmer/end user, etc) name?
* is the user allowed access to the system?
* what does the user want to do, and how often?
* are the user's jobs batch or online?
* what production data does the user want to access - in read or write mode, and does anyone else need to read the data?
* how much file storage is the user allowed to access?

Section 3
Planning for computer operations management

* can the user start prints?
* are large prints allowed?
* is there a limit on the resources allowed - paper, disk space, CPU usage, mainstore occupancy, tapes, elapsed time?
* is the user to be forced off the system if using too much resource; eg warned if using 50% over agreed amount, cut-off in flight if 100% over agreed amount?
* is the user going to be submitting jobs that will eventually go into production, ie is filestore to be allocated for both development and production work?

There must be a clear division between test, and production data and files. When there is a requirement to progress from test to live a formal procedure must apply. This procedure should include checking for evidence of adherence to operability standards and completion of acceptance testing. See 3.1.5 and the IT Infrastructure Library module on **Software Control & Distribution** for further information.

3.1.8.13 Media provision

The Ops Manager must ensure there is sufficient stock of all necessary print and media requirements within Ops. This stock should cover:

* magnetic tapes
* data cartridges
* stationery
* printer ribbons
* toner
* any other miscellaneous supplies including cleaning materials.

Ops may also have to provide media for the users. A decision on this needs to be made when the SLAs are formulated.

Magnetic tapes, especially, wear out with constant use. Tapes should be cleaned regularly. Magnetic tape cleaning devices can be hired or purchased for this purpose. When monitored failure rates reach a set level the tapes should be replaced.

A proper stock control procedure needs to be written, which should include supplies for the users, if applicable. The amount of stationery used gives a good indication of how often it needs to be ordered. Stationery should be ordered when, or before, a minimum stock level is reached. The minimum stock level should be based on previous usage levels for the length of time it normally takes the contractor to deliver that particular item of stationery. Workload peaks and expected growth should be taken into account before finalizing minimum stock levels.

There needs to be an adequate stock of miscellaneous supplies such as printer ribbons, tape unit cleaners, toners and screen cleaners. The IT Directorate might also supply the users with ribbons for PC printers and with screen cleaners. A minimum stock level should be decided upon and maintained.

All of the above media supplies need to be catered for at the disaster backup site, if applicable. Again, a minimum stock level should be maintained and checked regularly, especially after any tests.

3.1.8.14 System running and closedown

Although most computer systems are up and running constantly, there are some systems that are powered off and on at weekends and/or overnight, or for housekeeping. The hardware supplier should be consulted for advice on whether the frequency of powering on and off the equipment is likely to have any adverse effects. Procedures should then be written covering how to perform the housekeeping, how often, and when it is best to power on and off the equipment so that the provision of an IT service to users, in accordance with SLAs, is least at risk. Similar procedures need to be in place for closing down air conditioning, power plant, etc and for switching on background heat.

Note that some of the larger systems can have quite complex IPL procedures and in these cases it can be a risk to let too long a period pass without all relevant Ops staff practising the IPL process. The risk is potentially greater where a shift pattern is worked which involves staff in lengthy breaks from work. In this situation it is a good idea for each shift to perform a weekly IPL, at the weekend if possible, to ensure that all staff are familiar and confident with this critical process.

Section 3
Planning for computer operations management

There may be times when the parameters within the operating system need to be changed. If these changes can be done while the system is up, but unused, so much the better. If not, the system has to be taken down, the parameters changed, and the system reloaded. System changes must be implemented in accordance with change management procedures.

When powered up, the system and associated hardware needs monitoring constantly. Increasingly this can be done by the operating system; and the hardware can be 'monitored' by itself and/or from a vendor's support centre. Incipient hardware faults are often fixed by engineers before they cause an incident. Only exceptions from expected system behaviour need to be dealt with by Ops. Unexpected console messages need to be checked using the suppliers' message manuals and dealt with according to laid-down procedures ie according to suppliers' recommendations.

There are various packages available from third parties that monitor the behaviour of computers and peripherals. The suppliers of the organization's main computer hardware and software should be consulted to confirm whether the required monitoring facilities are available within the organization's existing systems and if not, that the data interfaces needed by third party packages are available. Suppliers may advise on the suitability of packages under consideration and be able to recommend one. The hardware engineer and software support staff should be consulted and asked to specify any information they need from a package to aid problem solving. It is recommended that preference is given to packages that clearly indicate exception conditions and wherever possible suggest corrective action.

If there is a major problem with the operating system or hardware it may need to be closed down. The procedure for this needs to be defined and the circumstances that would precede this close down need to be documented thoroughly. On the other hand the system may fail or close untidily. In both circumstances system recovery procedures should include:

* the involvement of problem management/vendor support as required

* instructions for starting up again

* how to bring up associated software (packages used, etc).

All incidents affecting the computer systems should be handled via the problem management process, and the Help Desk must be informed immediately.

All procedures described in this section must be thoroughly tested.

The IT Infrastructure Library **Contingency Planning** module covers the procedures for disaster recovery.

3.1.8.15 Transaction Processing (online) systems

The target availability of the online systems is documented in the SLAs. The procedures for Ops must cover the following aspects for each online system.

Start-up

Instructions to guide operators during the start-up process must be provided - these are written by the TP support staff. An example statement:

> "if this is the first start-up of the day the response to message x is y. For subsequent start ups the response is z."

As the system has to be up by a certain time, the average length of time the start-up procedure takes needs to be documented; for example:

> "the transaction processing system takes approximately one hour to bring up fully. As the system has to be up by 7 am, the start-up procedure must be commenced by 5.30 to allow 30 minutes' leeway for any incidents. Any delay in the start of the system, or any incidents during the start-up, must be reported to the Help Desk immediately and must be thoroughly investigated, and documented records on how to avoid a recurrence must be produced. Laid-down problem management procedures must at all times be adhered to."

Closedown

The closedown procedures should cover the following:

* how to close down the system
* what messages are expected
* what the responses to enter are
* how to deal with unexpected responses.

Closedown procedures should be based on the supplier's technical manuals for the system and any variations should be clearly documented.

Section 3
Planning for computer operations management

The procedures should cover the backing-up of the system, which should be done as frequently as necessary, but as a minimum prior to, or immediately after, closing the online service. By doing backups at this point, the operators can return the system to its state of closedown at any time. This helps if there are any problems during overnight processing.

An SLA may contain a condition whereby, if the need arises, the users can extend the length of time a particular IT service is to be provided. In such a case the users should inform Ops as soon as possible of any necessary extension. Extensions should be controlled through the Help Desk if it is in operation. The procedures for the operators to follow when there are extensions to the online system must be included in the Ops manual.

Monitoring the online system

An online system needs to be monitored constantly during the available periods - 3.1.10.1 contains guidance on items to be monitored. If monitoring software is used at the site, instructions on how to use the software should be included in the general online procedures, using the supplier's technical manuals as a guide.

Emergency start-up procedures

If an online system fails, an emergency start-up procedure is needed to cover any different parameters that need to be used. (For instance database recovery needs to be handled carefully.) In general, it is best to automate this emergency start-up procedure so that there is less opportunity for errors to be made. The operators should inform the Help Desk of any problems with availability during the agreed times.

Changes to the online systems

Any changes to the online systems should be implemented as instructed by the change management process, under configuration management control. A copy of the change management manual should be kept in Ops for staff to refer to.

3.1.8.16 Backup and restoration

A proper backup strategy needs to be set up. For example:

> "All system software and application software, all program and job control libraries, and all data in the operating environment must be backed up. These backups must happen on a regular basis to support the reliability and availability criteria defined in Service Level Agreements and the disaster procedures."

The backup strategy also decides the way the backups are created. Whether the backups are by whole or part disk volumes or by individual files depends on the operating environment, the time it takes to do the backups and the backup packages used.

Data cartridges can be used to create whole volume backups each night. Magnetic tapes, being slower, may only be able to back up individual files, or selected volumes each night.

The backups and restores of system and application software and of libraries should be separate from the backups and restores of data. The data backups are normally provided within jobs, by the retention of previous versions or copying of current versions of files. Software and library backups must be explicitly scheduled. The complete software item or library should be backed up, rather than just the parts that have been changed since the last backup. The schedule for backing up files and volumes must be fully documented, properly maintained and adequately safeguarded as the contents of the schedule are required for disaster recovery purposes.

OSG are involved in setting the backup strategy as they have the experience to comment on any technical constraints imposed by the hardware and/or software being used. Once the strategy is agreed the job of implementing it, eg coding JCL, establishing procedures for managing the magnetic media, and implementing software tools, can be carried out by OSG. Their responsibilities must be clearly spelt out in the Ops manual.

It is important that, if the operators do not work on public holidays or other specially designated days, any backups that fall on those days are transferred to the previous or following day. For example, at Easter the Friday backups should be transferred to Thursday and the Monday backups to Tuesday. This rescheduling is to avoid backups being missed and the backup schedule going awry.

All system and application software should additionally be backed up as part of normal change management immediately prior to and immediately after any change takes place, for example Program Temporary Fixes(PTFs) or configuration changes. This backup caters for any problems during the change and also means that if the system fails after the second backup, the change does not need to be applied again.

Section 3
Planning for computer operations management

All backup and restore programs for each job and system should be tested prior to Ops' acceptance. For further information please read the IT Infrastructure Library modules on **Testing Software for Operational Use** and **Availability Management**.

Restore procedures must include provision for any security packages used in the installation. With some security packages restoration is impossible without the user passwords, which Ops should not know. For example, if a user password is needed out of office hours to restore a file, the Security and the Ops Managers have to be informed. They provide the passwords needed. In these circumstances, the user must be informed that the password has been used and should change it at the earliest opportunity.

3.1.8.17 Environment

Detailed guidance on all the environmental topics covered in this section is available in the Environmental Sets of the IT Infrastructure Library. The responsibility for planning and implementing this guidance sometimes lies outside Ops. This section highlights the activities that are most likely to be the responsibility of Ops or to require its input. Any incidents/problems connected with any of the environmental areas should be reported via the problem management system.

Power

If Ops is responsible for any actions with respect to the power supply, eg monitoring it, taking remedial action in the event of a break, procedures need to be included in the Ops manual.

The power supply is usually monitored by voltage and frequency monitors installed in the power distribution unit (PDU). Alarms are triggered when preset levels are exceeded. Procedures should be written covering what action Ops needs to take in the event of the alarm sounding. The details for these procedures should be based on information contained in the PDU supplier's manuals. Computers may well suffer from power spikes and therefore the computer suppliers' manuals could also be relevant. Applications recovery may be required (see 3.1.5.1).

Air conditioning

The supplier's manuals are probably highly technical; so the relevant details, for example on monitoring, need to be rewritten into the Ops manual. If the air conditioning unit needs maintenance from the operators, such as changing

51

filters, this maintenance needs to be included in the procedures together with instructions on how to order additional parts.

If there is a 24-hour security guard in the building, it is recommended that an air conditioning control panel be situated in the security area. This panel would immediately indicate to the security guards if there was an air conditioning problem affecting the computer room. Instructions must be provided on whom to contact to deal with the problem.

Humidity

Humidity in the computer room needs to be controlled. An atmosphere that is too dry promotes static electricity. There should be humidity monitoring equipment, which is normally linked to the air conditioning units.

If humidity monitoring is an Ops' responsibility, the Ops manual must contain procedures for using the monitoring equipment to check humidity and dealing with any abnormal conditions. The monitoring equipment manufacturer's manual should be the source of these procedures.

Within the procedures there should be a warning that if static electricity exceeds normal tolerances, it must be reported via the problem management system so that steps can be taken to remedy it. There are anti-static aerosol sprays and floor mats that can be used to reduce the risk of static problems and these solutions should be actioned through the building manager.

Fire system

Advice on fire detection and suppression systems is available in the **Fire Precautions in IT Installations** module of the Environmental Management Set of the IT Infrastructure Library.

Whatever system is used Ops will be responsible for implementing procedures to be followed in the event of a fire; eg evacuation procedures, use of emergency exit points, use of fire extinguishers, contacting emergency services. These procedures must be included in the Ops manual and displayed publicly as stipulated in the appropriate legal requirements.

Dust control

The amount of dust in the computer room needs to be monitored. For the more highly-sensitive equipment, dust extraction points may be needed in the room. These provide a method of cleaning the floor of the room without stirring up the dust, which could cause disk errors and other problems.

Section 3
Planning for computer operations management

Whether office cleaning personnel are allowed in the computer area may be dictated by security conditions. If they are not, the procedures for dealing with room cleaning need to be included in the general operating procedures. However, it is recommended that specialist computer room cleaning companies are used.

The void under the false floor, if applicable, should be cleaned twice a year at least. The timing of cleaning should be documented in the Ops manual, and organized with the Security Manager if clearance is required.

Anti-static and dust removal mats can be used to alleviate dust problems. If these need to be changed by Ops, the length of use and the ordering of new ones should be written in the procedures.

3.1.8.18 Maintenance of computer hardware

Cleaning and other DIY maintenance

To ensure reliable operation, regular cleaning needs to be performed on all magnetic tape devices, data cartridge units and printers. Ops may also be responsible for the maintenance of users' equipment; eg PCs and PC printers. If this is the case, the procedures and timing for this activity need to be documented.

The suppliers of the peripherals should be consulted about the maintenance required. The suppliers should provide manuals, as part of the contract conditions, showing how to maintain the equipment, and the frequency of cleaning related to usage.

The Ops manual should contain procedures, based on information contained in the suppliers' manuals, on all maintenance to be performed by the Ops staff. Diagrams of the peripherals, showing unfamiliar parts, should be included.

Magnetic-tape devices need cleaning using special cleaning fluid and lint-free cloth; these consumables can normally be provided by the suppliers.

Data-cartridge devices should be cleaned using a special cleaning cartridge. Some data-cartridge devices actually stop working until they have been cleaned (a sensor measures how often they have been used).

The printers should be cleaned using a vacuum cleaner to remove any paper dust. Cleaners are sometimes built-in on larger line printers. Some laser printers need regular maintenance by the Ops staff. Others just need maintenance from the engineers.

Printer ribbons and toner cartridges need replacing regularly. Some printers automatically send a message when the toner needs replacing. Ribbons need replacing before the print produced is too faint for the quality agreed in the SLAs.

Scheduled maintenance

Pre-arranged visits by the customer engineer need to be planned. These visits allow the engineer periodically to replace items such as tape heads, drive belts, etc before they wear out. The maintenance timetable needs to be agreed with users and should preferably be recorded in SLAs. The IT system may be unavailable to users during the maintenance. If possible, this maintenance should be performed out of office hours. However, organizations need to balance the cost against the benefits, as out-of-hours maintenance can be expensive. Laser printers, magnetic tape units, data cartridge devices and robots, if used, are the peripherals most commonly maintained by the customer engineers.

Unscheduled maintenance

If a hardware device fails, unscheduled maintenance may be required. Ops needs to agree with the IT Services Manager the conditions relating to the release of equipment for unscheduled maintenance as the SLAs could be affected. These conditions should be documented in the Ops manual.

Maintenance problems

Any problems with maintenance of the computer equipment must be reported and dealt with via the problem management system. The Ops staff must be aware of the terms of maintenance contracts with suppliers and engineers. Any differences in the interpretation of terms of contracts, between Ops and a contractor, must also be reported and dealt with via the problem management system.

3.1.8.19 Systems programming

Although it may appear more natural for Systems Programming(SP) to be associated with applications programming, their 'closeness' to the machines and their work with the operating system(OS) make it more practical for this function to report to the IT Services Manager, possibly via Ops.

An example job description for a systems programmer is contained in Annex B.

Section 3
Planning for computer operations management

SP can be broken down into the following major areas. SP is primarily concerned with supporting operating system and similar software in the same kind of way that applications programmers and analysts support the business applications that run on the IT system.

Software installation This encompasses the installation, maintenance and customization, under configuration management control, of the operating system. For software such as third party tools (schedulers, tape managers etc) it may be appropriate for SP to install the products, leaving implementation, ie how they will be used, to OSG.

Problem resolution This involves investigating OS software incidents and problems, debugging where appropriate and/or applying fixes from software suppliers. This function normally involves a great deal of liaison between several groups and must therefore be effectively managed, under the control of the problem management function.

System tuning In conjunction with capacity management staff, SP ensures all OS software is appropriately tuned to provide optimum performance from the hardware and software. This tuning activity takes into account workload profiles and SLAs.

Technical consultancy SP are the OS software experts within the installation and as such they provide a technical consultancy and advisory role to Ops and Applications Managers.

3.1.9 Security

Security is an increasingly vital area in IT owing to the growing use of computing in all business spheres. Data and equipment are open to undesirable manipulation and destruction that could have wide ranging repercussions, either financially or in terms of political or business integrity. Ops is invariably closest to the main data and equipment and hence needs very sound security arrangements.

Organizations should consider carrying out a risk assessment exercise. Details of the CCTA Risk Analysis and Management Method CRAMM are available from CCTA.

For more information on IT security, please consult CCTA IS Guide C4 on Security and Privacy and the CCTA Security Library. Government organizations should consult their Departmental and IT Security Officer for advice.

The IT Infrastructure Library
Computer Operations Management

3.1.9.1 Physical access security

The whole Ops working area should be a secure area, accessible only by authorized staff. The Ops Manager should maintain a list of the staff authorized to gain access. For remote sites under the management of Ops, authorized user staff, suitably trained, should be included on the list.

Levels of access and separate access zones are recommended where installations deal with data or equipment that is in any way business or politically sensitive. An example of who should be admitted to various zones is given in Annex D.

In installations that are of particular sensitivity, accesses to sensitive areas must be recorded and regularly reviewed. Recording and review must be done in addition to security vetting.

In any installation, out-of-hours access to secure areas should be noted, particularly where media use or retrieval is involved. The reason for access should be noted. The access log should be reviewed daily and any unusual accesses investigated.

3.1.9.2 Access control systems

There are a number of ways in which access to restricted areas can be controlled. They should be used in conjunction with the recommendations in 3.1.9.1. The options include:

*   security guard - having a permanent guard on the access door(s) who controls and records all accesses

*   general restriction locks - ordinary locks to which authorized staff have a duplicate key, keypad entry lock with a common number for entry, remotely-operated locks with single access-code

*   specific restriction locking systems - locks with selective access restriction and multi-level individual access tokens/cardkeys, individual number/password access, state-of-the-art physical characteristic access authorization (hand, voice, fingerprint, etc).

Section 3
Planning for computer operations management

All these systems can provide invaluable help in restricting unauthorized access. Selection criteria for your site should be developed and these include:

* cost
* hands-free
* site sensitivity
* number of users
* size/location of access point(s)
* maintenance/reliability issues
* system upgradeability.

Each site's selection criteria should be checklisted and prospective vendors asked to respond to the list.

3.1.9.3 Magnetic media security

All magnetic media should be held within the controlled access area when not in use and be stored in racking where absences can be easily and rapidly spotted.

There should be secure locations for live-data backup files. These locations invariably are:

* fireproof safe - for immediate storage after backup
  - to provide local recovery/restore (where online backup files are not used)
  - to provide temporary storage for media being removed and stored offsite to aid disaster recovery
* offsite store - every installation must have an offsite data store in which data is stored, to be used for recovery in the event of a disaster. The media should arrive at the offsite store as soon as is practical, but no later than 24 hours after creation. For precise details of the features and contents of the offsite store, please refer to the IT Infrastructure Library module on **Contingency Planning**.

3.1.9.4 Stationery security

Computer stationery needs to be controlled both before (in the case of blank drafts, orders, cheques etc) and after printing. See also 3.1.8.7 - 3.1.8.9.

Disposal of unwanted printout

Storage and disposal of unwanted print should be performed either in Ops using a secure media store and shredder, or by an approved and security-vetted (if appropriate) contractor.

3.1.9.5 General security for Operations

Much of the security required in the Ops area is common sense. There should be, for example, standing instructions for shift management to:

* ensure that hardware cabinets are kept locked when not being maintained
* challenge any unrecognized intruders
* ensure that all access control systems work - doors close correctly, etc
* carry out random checks on media library
* randomly check special stationery store security
* report any suspicious incidents to Security and record in the shift log
* ensure all visitors are accompanied at all times.

These activities take little time and help safeguard the integrity of the installation.

3.1.10 Measuring Operations' efficiency and effectiveness

The Ops area is crucial in the service delivery process. Ops has an important part to play in meeting IT service requirements. Typically, Ops is required to provide IT services that:

* offer a stable online window for the prescribed hours
* allow that window to present users with current and backed up data on time each day (achieved by suitably organizing batch schedules)

Section 3
Planning for computer operations management

* are able to cope with the additional peaks that critical business periods in various applications demand

* deliver prints to locations by specific deadlines

* maintain a reliable IT service environment and meet the processing targets.

Meeting these IT service requirements involves many IT Directorate functions outside Ops, as described in other IT Infrastructure Library modules.

It is, however, essential that the efficiency and effectiveness of Ops at providing IT services - how well it carries out its responsibilities for successfully delivering IT services that meet service requirements, and with what resources - can be measured. This information is used to highlight areas for quality improvement and to show when quality improvements take place. The Ops Manager must exercise continuous control over the quality of operations using as a guideline the measures described in this section and in 5.1.3. Any deficiencies must be traced back to source and put right to prevent recurrence. The urgency with which corrective action is required depends on the severity of the problem - the targets set for the organization's problem management system should be used.

Some indicators of Ops' effectiveness at providing IT services follow (note that factors outside Ops' control will have to be disentangled):

* system and service consistently available on time (or, if not, for reasons outside the responsibilities of Ops) - eg measure frequency and severity of late starts

* data input and work run according to schedule and prints despatched on time - eg measure

  - percentage of late inputs

  - percentage of failures attributable to input data

  - percentage of critical path checkpoints met

  - percentage of required volume of work processed

  - percentage of reports delivered on time

  - input data volumes processed by period

  - number of reports printed and distributed by period

59

The IT Infrastructure Library
Computer Operations Management

* few incidents caused by Ops, and none serious - eg measure the percentage reruns and reprints attributable to Ops errors

* incidents that Ops handle are dealt with quickly and in accordance with the problem management system - eg measure the percentage of incidents and problems closed within timescale

* adherence to budgets.

Ops' efficiency can ultimately be gauged by the amount of work processed per staff member - but care must be taken to isolate factors outside Ops' control. The automation of Ops can, for example, result in efficiency and effectiveness improvements, but Ops may have to bid competitively for funds to automate functions.

These measures are typical of those required in most Ops areas. Installations should define their own measures to reflect their service requirements and any special management needs. A good problem management system (see the IT Infrastructure Library **Help Desk** and **Problem Management** modules) gives comprehensive information on service quality and helps isolate incidents caused by Ops errors, to give clear measures of Ops' effectiveness at providing IT services.

The following subsections gives details on aspects of IT service monitoring that can be used as a basis for further measuring the efficiency and effectiveness of Ops. Guidance is provided to help organizations achieve high levels of efficiency and effectiveness.

Guidance on management reviews of the efficiency and effectiveness of the Ops function is given in section 5.1.3.

3.1.10.1 Online service

The key measure that determines whether the online service is a success is that it meets its SLA. To do this, it needs to meet the set availability target for the online window, be up on time each day and meet the demands set for response time. See the IT Infrastructure Library module on **Service Level Management** for further details.

Ops can have a crucial effect on availability; for example the time to restore normal service after an incident is often entirely in its hands. Operating procedures must be explicit and must emphasize the need for speed.

Section 3
Planning for computer operations management

Ops should ensure that the elements within its control operate effectively to meet the service targets. The following areas demand close control.

Online day start-up
A check should be kept on the time start-up is achieved each day. Some contingency is required between start-up and the actual online start time in the SLA to give a recovery opportunity if problems arise. In general an hour is sufficient. If this time is eroding, it gives early warning that action, for example concerning batch capacity or rescheduling, is needed. It has been proved over many years that this is the time of day when Ops are at their most vulnerable in providing a service to users.

Online performance
This is the most visible area of service and hence sometimes the most sensitive with customers. Regular monitoring of the online service should normally be carried out by the Capacity Manager. The Capacity Manager may delegate some or all the monitoring responsibilities to Ops. Regular monitoring should be carried out using performance monitoring and accounting facilities on a retrospective basis and an online system monitoring tool to give an indication on a snapshot basis. This monitoring enables performance problems to be identified and addressed rapidly. Areas of particular focus are:

* CPU utilization
* channel utilization
* disk I/O rates
* transaction volumes/throughput
* hardware/environment failure.

Where appropriate, Ops needs to act, normally by alerting the Capacity Manager, whenever the monitoring shows that service levels are threatened by any of the above factors. If the problem is of Ops' making, eg too much batch work scheduled, Ops needs to rectify the situation.

Network
Also of significance to the quality of online service is the network. Problems relating to the network have a significant effect on online service and Ops should notify perceived problems to the network control staff quickly. This notification should act only as additional information since network control constantly monitor the network. See the IT Infrastructure Library module on **Network Management** for more information.

3.1.10.2 Batch work performance

Each batch session needs to be examined for both the whole portfolio of applications and individual ones. A critical path should be established for each night's session that is essential to complete housekeeping, key processing and online start up. This path should then be checkpointed with timebands within which identified stages of processing should be reached to keep to schedule. Actual performance can then be gauged against these checkpoints.

A simple example:

	Planned Critical Path	Actual
20.00	Online window shuts	20.10
20.15	Main shutdown complete	20.30
21.30	File backups complete	21.50
21.45	Main file update begins	22.15
23.00	File update complete	23.30
23.00	File sorting runs start	23.35
00.50	File sorts end	01.30
00.50	Main posting run start	01.30
01.30	End posting	02.15
01.45	Start report runs	02.30
04.00	End reports	05.00
04.30	Batch validation run ends	05.30
04.45	Open online files	05.45
05.00	Check online files/facilities	06.00
05.15	Online window available	06.15
08.00	Users start online use	07.45.

This simple example shows how a minor slippage in a batch run can reduce the contingency prior to online start up. Regular slippages noted by this method, as well as any other problems, should have their cause determined and action taken to avoid recurrences that have an impact on the service, through the problem management system.

3.1.10.3 Peak service periods

The periods of extra service demand due to business peaks should be monitored. Ops must adhere to peak-time schedules (laid down in the SLAs). Any incident - including

Section 3
Planning for computer operations management

deviations from peak-time schedules - caused by Ops is an Ops quality problem. Any problem caused by SLAs being unworkable, or the workload being greater than specified in the SLA, should be tackled by the Service Level Manager. If peak-time targets are not met on a regular basis, Ops procedures should be examined to determine whether Ops is responsible and corrective action should be taken. If Ops is not responsible, the SLA should be used as a vehicle to determine action; eg do we need to increase capacity for a once-a-month peak, or can we reschedule other work to make more room? Monitoring data, produced by the capacity management team or under delegated authority by Ops, is used as input to the decision-making process on this matter.

3.1.10.4 Print

SLAs determine what prints are to be delivered, where, and by what time. The output control process monitors Ops' success in achieving delivery targets. Timings are recorded for each job for the following events:

* print job end
* print in print queue
* print printed
* print ready for dispatch
* print dispatched
* print delivered (and possibly signed for).

Printing done remotely can be monitored in much the same way, the delivery point probably being the print queue.

Printing times must be reviewed against the SLA targets, and any deviations explained and rectified at source by whichever function is responsible for the deviation.

Ops' effectiveness is measured by adherence to print schedules. As adherence to print schedules is the second most visible of Ops' service provision tasks, it should have high priority placed on it. (Too often Ops views print as 'lowly' work and as a result Ops' image as well as its effectiveness suffers.)

3.1.10.5 Hardware and environment

The Ops physical environment is vulnerable to failure, just as the hardware itself is.

If responsibility for monitoring the environmental controls is vested in Ops, it needs to set up checks in the following areas:

* power supply
* temperature/humidity and dust
* water leakage
* hardware maintenance schedule
* peripheral cleaning
* stationery.

Ops' effectiveness in this area is gauged by the speed with which problems with the hardware and environment are reported and any corrective actions that are Ops' responsibility are taken.

3.1.10.6 Incident control

Ops is responsible for the control of incidents that arise within its domain. All incidents that cannot be resolved are passed to the problem management team for resolution. The use of a single problem management system for all incidents ensures they are handled and recorded in a coherent way. When Ops discovers a fault in processing or any other aspect of its work, an incident report must be raised. Incidents need not have an impact on the IT service directly. Something that could be done better in the future to make Ops' life easier can be addressed as an incident.

The Ops Manager should encourage staff to report often and honestly on anything out of the ordinary. In this way, the Ops Manager can keep abreast of what is happening in the Ops process and get advance warning of any problems.

Ops' effectiveness can be measured using the following metrics:

* how few incidents are caused by Ops
* how many incidents (that sensibly could be) are spotted by Ops prior to a user query

Section 3
Planning for computer operations management

* how well Ops resolves incidents that are under Ops' control, eg

    - mean elapsed time to achieve incident resolution, broken down by impact code (are resolution times within target?)

    - percentage of incidents closed by Ops without reference to other support groups.

For further information on incident control see 3.1.4.1 and the IT Infrastructure Library module on **Problem Management**.

3.1.10.7 Efficiency and effectiveness - general

Section 3.1.10 has given some guidance on monitoring whether Ops plays a positive role in the service delivery process and helping to ensure it plays such a role. For many of the areas highlighted, tools are available to automate much of the required checking - network monitoring and print monitoring for example. These tools should be used to help Ops play its part in meeting the SLA targets. See section 7 of this module for further information on the facilities required of some classes of tools.

In all of the areas highlighted, common sense determines the best measures for your site. Select measures that clearly show success, failure or improvements taking place - and that do not have a heavy overhead, manual or system.

3.1.11 Management reviews and audits

Plans must be made for regular management reviews of the Ops function, and for audits to check that it is adhering to laid-down procedures. See 5.1.2 to 5.1.6 for more details.

3.2 Dependencies

3.2.1 Hardware and software tools

Ops is becoming increasingly dependent on tools. In some installations these tools are PC-based. It is essential that organizations plan the processes, by which the tools and PCs are identified, purchased and installed, to ensure that required tools are in place in advance of Ops needing them.

To select tools, a detailed requirement statement should be drawn up and the relevant manufacturers of hardware and software approached to provide products that meet that

The IT Infrastructure Library
Computer Operations Management

specification. Selection should ultimately be based on the best cost/functionality mix. For more details on tools see section 7.

3.2.2 Documentation

Well defined and up to date documentation is necessary to ensure that Ops functions effectively, that systems can be understood and that changes can be accommodated with minimum disruption to the service.

Good documentation provides the following benefits:

* increased guidance for Ops
* more maintainable systems
* easier enhancements
* better training for Ops.

The documentation used by Ops can usually be classified according to its source; eg the hardware and software vendors, applications systems development, in-house specialist and technical support, and Ops' own.

3.2.2.1 Hardware and software vendors

It is essential that Ops have their own up-to-date copies of the relevant technical manuals for all the operating system software and hardware that they are expected to use in running or monitoring the computer systems. It is recommended that there is a nominated person with a responsibility for ensuring that Ops has this documentation. This could be a job that rotates through each shift over a period.

Obtaining vendor-prepared documentation is not generally a problem; however the quality of the documentation provided can vary considerably, and there can be long lead-times.

3.2.2.2 Application systems

There should be operating instructions for each application system that is run. Instructions for each system can be divided into the following sections.

System summary

Provides a basic description of the system's overall purpose as well as its primary functional components and their relationships. It is helpful if it includes relevant diagrams and/or flowcharts.

Detailed system flowcharts	Shows all programs, files and (possibly) online terminals.
Preprocessing	Describes necessary hardware and software resources, required input files, output formats and scheduling parameters.
Processing	Details processing procedures and explains all status and exception messages that may be received.
Postprocessing	Describes closedown procedures (in the case of online systems), end of processing activities and end of run control total calculations. Also describes all offline processing.
Backup & restart procedures	Describes backup procedures for critical files and restart of processing using these backups.

The job documentation should be provided in a common layout. For example, page 1 is always the job description, page 2 always contains the flowcharts, etc. With this standard layout, information can be obtained easily and problems solved more quickly.

There are packages available that produce the documentation needed from programs as they are written. See section 7 for more details. At many sites, the documentation is the last thing to be written, if it is at all, when in fact it should be drafted during the design stage. Any packages that automate this task should be considered seriously.

3.2.2.3 Technical support manual

The contents of this manual will depend to a great extent on Ops' responsibilities in the installation. If Ops is expected to monitor the network, even just out of normal office hours, Ops should have current documentation on the network configuration. Likewise any routines or programs developed for Ops' use by areas such as systems programming should be documented using the same standard as for applications systems.

3.2.2.4 Ops (including OSG) manual

See Annex C.

3.2.2.5 Documentation provision

For application systems documentation and specialist/technical support documentation there are two major challenges:

* getting the documentation in the first place
* ensuring that it is maintained.

The first challenge can be tackled by making the provision of adequate documentation part of the process by which a new system is implemented. Keeping it up to date can be encouraged by asking the originator to sign a statement that a program change does not require corresponding documentation change if no documentation updates are provided. If nothing else, this approach will protect Ops from unfair criticism in the event of a later problem.

The provision of up-to-date documentation is a fundamental part of the overall change management process; the organization's change management procedures must ensure that required documentation changes are actually made.

3.2.2.6 Documentation standards

After the required documents are identified, documentation standards must be established to guide documentation activities and to evaluate results. These standards fall into two areas, those related to content and those governing format.

In terms of content, documentation must be:

* accurate
* complete
* clear
* concise.

Accuracy and completeness can be assessed by those familiar with the application system. Clarity is best evaluated by someone unfamiliar with the system but who will be expected to use the documentation. Conciseness can be checked by determining whether or not the information is actually needed and whether the same information can be put across more succinctly as a list or table.

Section 3
Planning for computer operations management

The documentation format standards are based on these criteria:

* ease of reference
* ease of use
* ease of maintenance.

The information that identifies the document must be easy to locate. For ease of use a document's contents can be segmented and sequenced in a practical and logical manner. Ease of maintenance can be ensured by using modular loose-leafed formats allowing each section to be easily updated or replaced.

3.2.3 Accommodation

3.2.3.1 Operations Bridge

An Operations Bridge is based on a similar concept to that of a ship's bridge, whereby the staff controlling the various IT systems are located in one place, physically separated from the equipment running the systems. The control room also includes facilities to monitor power and environmental conditions.

The elimination of the need to have staff permanently located with the equipment allows some relaxation in the environmental tolerances of the machine room (eg lighting, noise levels and draughts) as well as the possibility of enhancing staff job satisfaction. Figure 4 gives a diagrammatic layout of an Operations Bridge.

Figure 4: Operations Bridge

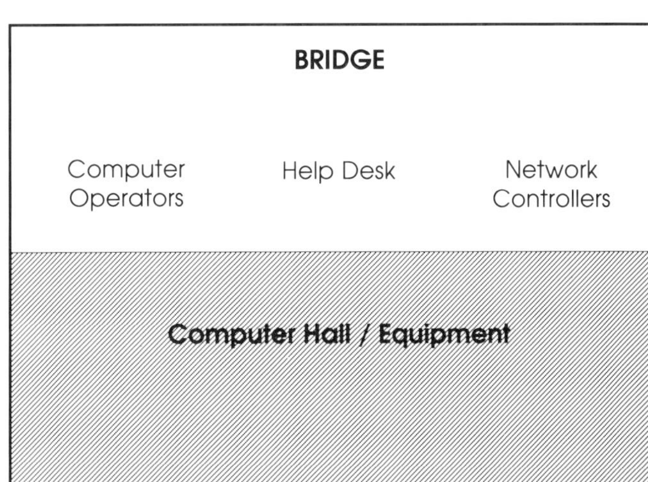

```
+---------------------------------------------------+
|                    BRIDGE                         |
|                                                   |
|   Computer         Help Desk        Network       |
|   Operators                         Controllers   |
|---------------------------------------------------|
|////////////////////////////////////////////////// |
|////////////  Computer Hall / Equipment  /////////|
|////////////////////////////////////////////////// |
|////////////////////////////////////////////////// |
+---------------------------------------------------+
```

A Bridge can be planned such that the hardware which is least likely to need attention is placed in a separate (unattended) room. The unattended room contains the CPU and fixed disk units. Ideally, this unattended room has its own environmental-control systems (fire detection/ suppression and air conditioning) with a control panel within the Bridge.

If separate areas deal with tape/data cartridge loading and output distribution, all the media hardware (tape/data cartridge machines, including cartridge robots) and printers can be in separate rooms. These rooms also have their own environmental control systems, and can have two panels, one in the Bridge and one in the loading/distribution areas.

Each separate zone that is not manned can be scanned by remote cameras, which helps ensure physical security of the zones.

Ideally the Bridge contains the computer operators and consoles, together with the network controllers and the Help Desk. The advantage of having these functions together is the ease of communication among them, particularly concerning incidents and problems. This fosters the provision of better services to the users. Care must be taken to ensure that work disciplines do not become lax. For instance, it would be very easy for the operators to tell the Help Desk about an incident without recording it in the problem management system.

The Bridge concept also lends itself to the control and operation from the bridge of a number of computers located centrally, not necessarily all from the same supplier, or a mix of central and remote computers and networks. This offers the prospect of higher Ops productivity.

The Bridge concept needs careful planning. It can embody a combination of any of the above ideas. The sort of Bridge implemented depends on the money, space and technology available.

3.2.3.2 Workstation planning

The planning of workstations for Ops staff is determined by a number of factors:

* available floorspace - layout and size of furniture are constrained by the floor area

* number of staff - obviously enough places for a workstation each is essential, with the possible

Section 3
Planning for computer operations management

exception of shift staff. Shift staff should at least have a lockable drawer for files etc. available to them, but may share workstations

* equipment type - the type and number of screens or consoles affect layout

* cabling and power outlets

* working relationships - workstations for related functions should be placed nearby if possible, and close to any access points; for example the Media Librarian near to the library.

In general, workstations should be designed to combine practical working space and filing capacity in a layout that creates a quality working environment for staff and equipment. More information on these subjects is contained in the IT Infrastructure Library Environmental modules entitled **The Office Environment & IT**, **Managing a Quality Working Environment for IT & Users**, **Office Design & Planning** and **Environmental Human Factors**.

3.2.3.3 Operators

If the operators have to work shifts, the accommodation needed is different from that if the operators work only days.

There needs to be a rest room for the operators to relax away from the noise and stress of the machine-room environment. The rest room could also be used as a meeting room. Within the rest room environment, there should be lockers for personal belongings.

For the shift workers, there needs to be provision for meals out of office hours. Provision should include, at least, a refrigerator, a microwave oven, cutlery, crockery and access to a sink.

3.2.3.4 Equipment engineers

Within the operations area, there may need to be provision for equipment engineers. Precise requirements are usually agreed during contractual negotiations. However, the requirements will normally include:

* office furniture, ie desk, cupboards

* a place to test equipment

* access to a telephone.

3.2.3.5 Media and stationery

Magnetic tapes, data cartridges and diskettes should be stored in an area or room with a controlled environment. The storage should be laid out in a way that eases access to media, and if possible makes the most used media the most accessible. As well as this, there needs to be a fire-proof safe for the storage of crucial data, eg last backup versions of master files. The fire-proof safe should, if possible, be protected by the organization's fire system.

Provision should also be made for offsite storage of backup copies of vital data, for use in case of disaster. The offsite storage area should be a safe distance from the main computer section.

The stationery required to service print requirements needs to be stored away from the peripherals due to dust and fire hazards. Only a bare minimum (eg 1-2 days stock) needs to be in the computer room at any one time. The paper-storage area needs to have fire-proof doors.

3.2.3.6 Access rules for support staff

Support staff comprising problem management and specialist support teams, system and application programmers, data control staff, the Media Librarian and others should not be allowed within any computer room. If a Bridge is set up, the same rules apply. Typically Help Desk and Network Control are then collocated with Ops.

If there is a problem requiring support staff to have access to the computer room/Bridge, there must be a security procedure, agreed by the Security Manager, to sign them in.

All the procedures covering access rules for support staff should be in the Ops manual, and tested and reviewed on a regular basis.

3.2.4 Adapting to change

The Ops area has evolved over the past 10-15 years from an unsophisticated production-line operation producing printout from batch runs using punched card input to its present form, responsible for providing a service to a vast audience of users in many locations and business sectors.

During this period, the role of Ops has changed relatively slowly in relation to the general advance of technology.

Section 3
Planning for computer operations management

The role of Ops is, however, now changing more rapidly. Many of the changes affect staff-skill requirements. Staff are the key to taking up new developments successfully and using them to the advantage of the business.

The changes described below are designed to make Ops more effective. They should be approached positively, with the full involvement of affected staff to ensure maximum success. Ops should involve other parts of the IT Directorate - they can probably help Ops to introduce the changes smoothly (see section 3.1.4).

3.2.4.1 The changes - and the response

The changes that are currently affecting, or soon will affect, Ops are as follows.

Customer service orientation

The IT Directorate is being viewed increasingly as a provider of service to organizations' business users and external customers. Ops plays a vital part in the provision of IT services to the users. Ops staff need to be aware of customer/service relationships and the contribution they are expected to make in supporting efforts to enhance IT services and customers' perception of the services. See related IT Infrastructure Library modules, particularly **Customer Liaison** and **Service Level Management**.

Automated or unattended operating

The most radical change affecting Ops is aimed at eliminating many of the 'human intervention' processes in the production cycle that have traditionally been carried out by operators. In practice, the adoption of automated or unattended operating almost invariably means that operators are presented with opportunities for self-development that would otherwise not have occurred. Section 3.3.1.4 covers these opportunities in more depth.

If it is planned to move to automated or unattended operating the organization must ensure the following areas can be effectively controlled without having staff in constant attendance:

* media handling
* scheduling
* support - probably switching the emphasis to on-call support
* security
* environment.

The IT Infrastructure Library
Computer Operations Management

Guidance on these areas, and on operability standards that make the tasks of Ops easier to automate, can be found in section 3.1 of this module. See also the IT Infrastructure Library **Unattended Operating** module.

Bridge

The central control of the day-to-day running of an organization's computers, networks and Help Desk from a 'nerve centre' or Bridge.

The Bridge is a practical way of grouping together key day-to-day staff and is a good way of helping to minimize staff shortage problems. Skills are invariably cross-fertilized in this environment. See 3.2.3.1 for more information.

3.3 People

When planning the Ops function, IT Services management should consult with staff and their representatives, eg the relevant trades unions.

3.3.1 Staffing

3.3.1.1 Numbers

Staffing of the Ops area is naturally dependent on the size and complexity of computing systems to be operated. The precise scope of Ops' responsibilities also has an influence - see 3.3.2. The chart below indicates typical staffing levels for various installation types.

	Type 1	**Type 2**	**Type 3**
Trainee Operator	2	3	4
Operator	1	3	4 to 8
Senior Operator	1	3	4 to 8
Shift Leader	2	3	4
Media Librarian	0	1	2
Data Control	2	5	6 to 10
Ops Analysts	1	3	5 to 8
Ops Manager	1	1	1

Type of site:

1: Mini or small mainframe based with 2 shifts running a mix of online and batch work.

2: Large or multiple mini or medium size mainframe site running 3 shifts with an extended online day and batch work.

3: Large mainframe site running a 24-hour, 6- or 7-days per week operation with long (maybe 24-hour) online window and significant volumes of batch work.

Section 3
Planning for computer operations management

These indicators are for guidance only and local judgement based on business criticality, type of applications and equipment, local working practices or constraints and legal implications is necessary. For example, employment legislation prevents the operation of equipment when there is no other person close by.

Many organizations save costs by not using trainee operators. However, organizations might benefit from reconsidering this policy as using trainee operators can provide a source of loyal, purpose-trained and available staff for a relatively low investment.

Ops areas are noted for the relatively high turnover of staff in certain regions. A policy for recruitment should be adopted that allows for this turnover. The use of trainees to complement the quota of experienced operators is an excellent way, where possible, of ensuring that staffing levels and workflow are not too disrupted. The recruitment policy should perhaps allow for additional recruitment when suitable candidates are found and use them as trainee or 'floating' operators. Although organizations need to operate within budgetary limits, they should not allow staff shortages to degrade the services.

3.3.1.2 Staff skills

The job descriptions in Annex B give a clear description of the various jobs within Ops. The types of skills sought in the various Ops positions are as follows.

Shift Leader/Operator/ Senior/Trainee Operator

These are usually shiftwork-based, so one of the prerequisites is that staff can work as part of a close-knit team. For all levels, a degree of technical aptitude is an advantage. Additionally, for the more senior positions look for the ability to lead a team and make decisions. Increasingly staff need to liaise with other sections within the IT Directorate and maybe even with users, so interpersonal skills are essential. All staff need to be able to work under pressure and to tight deadlines.

Media Librarian/ Data Control

These are largely clerical, with an element of technical knowledge required. Staff in these areas should be able to pay attention to detail, work to a defined timeframe, and be capable of liaising effectively with other parts of the organization.

Operations Analysts

Operations Analysts have a guiding role in the day-to-day running of Ops. They need to be technically skilled in the areas of operating-system control, application-job control,

The IT Infrastructure Library
Computer Operations Management

	utility packages, file and disk-storage management and scheduling. They need to have a degree of business understanding and the required interpersonal skills to liaise on Ops' behalf with other areas.
Systems Programmers	SPs need an in-depth technical knowledge of the internal structure and functionality of the operating system software. They also need strong analytical problem solving ability and well developed communication skills.
Ops Manager	See 3.1.1.
All staff	All the skills indicated are basic to the jobs in question. Additionally, staff are required to be flexible and adaptable. They should be trained in, and make it their business to become aware of, service and business issues, and be keen to learn in order to progress their careers.
	The development of unattended or automated operating should have the effect of making operators' jobs in particular less onerous physically - much of the manual intervention being removed. This change makes it essential that operators develop alternative skills - see 3.3.1.4 and 3.3.3.

3.3.1.3 Grading staff - job comparisons

The grading of staff in all Ops jobs, as for the Ops Manager (see 3.1.1), presents problems in terms of finding the correct level and 'status' for the job. Government departments can obtain grading standards from the Administration Group Grading Guides together with any special guidance published for the IT specialism. However, organizations may find the following generic guidance useful.

To help determine the level, the table below shows comparable jobs in other IT or user areas:

Trainee Operator	Data control clerk, general clerk
Operator	Senior clerk, junior programmer
Senior Operator	Clerical supervisor, programmer
Shift Leader	Senior programmer, small project leader, clerical manager
Media Librarian	Operator, senior clerk
Data Control	Trainee operator, general clerk
Ops Analysts	Senior programmer, small project leader, clerical manager
Ops Manager	Chief programmer, chief analyst, senior project manager, user section manager (eg Benefit Office Manager).

Section 3
Planning for computer operations management

This table can be used as a guide to relative grading and status. Each site differs in its precise make-up, but this guide provides a basic framework from which to develop.

3.3.1.4 Career planning

Major differences have always existed between the job requirements of operators and programmers. Many companies still require programmers to be educated to degree level or have previous DP experience. It is often still assumed that Ops staff can be found from within the organization's postroom.

Nowadays, some Ops staff are often expected to carry out sophisticated tasks, eg monitoring online systems, networks or systems performance and to play a key role in delivering IT services that meet SLAs. In short the job of many Ops staff is becoming more skilled and much more time is spent interfacing with sophisticated operating systems, monitors and Ops-related tools. The number of 'mundane' Ops jobs is tending to diminish. These changes make it important that attention is paid to career planning for Ops staff which in turn should make it easier to recruit and retain Ops staff of good calibre.

Figure 5, overleaf, shows an example career path for operators where the opportunities for more interesting work depend on moves to the technical support roles. In the case of a large shift environment, particularly, there are also likely to be opportunities to develop a career in managing people.

In the past, the two most common career aspirations for operators were eventual promotion to the position of Ops Manager or a transfer into programming. Today, IT Services offers a far greater choice including systems programming, operations analysis, network control, Help Desk, change management, problem management, security administration, and magnetic storage management.

3.3.2 Organization

Organization for Ops has two aspects: where Ops fits within the IT Directorate and how Ops itself is structured.

3.3.2.1 Operations within the IT Directorate

Ops has a key role in IT: it provides the 'production line' for the service that is to be delivered to the user or customer. The Ops Manager reports to the IT Services Manager.

The IT Infrastructure Library
Computer Operations Management

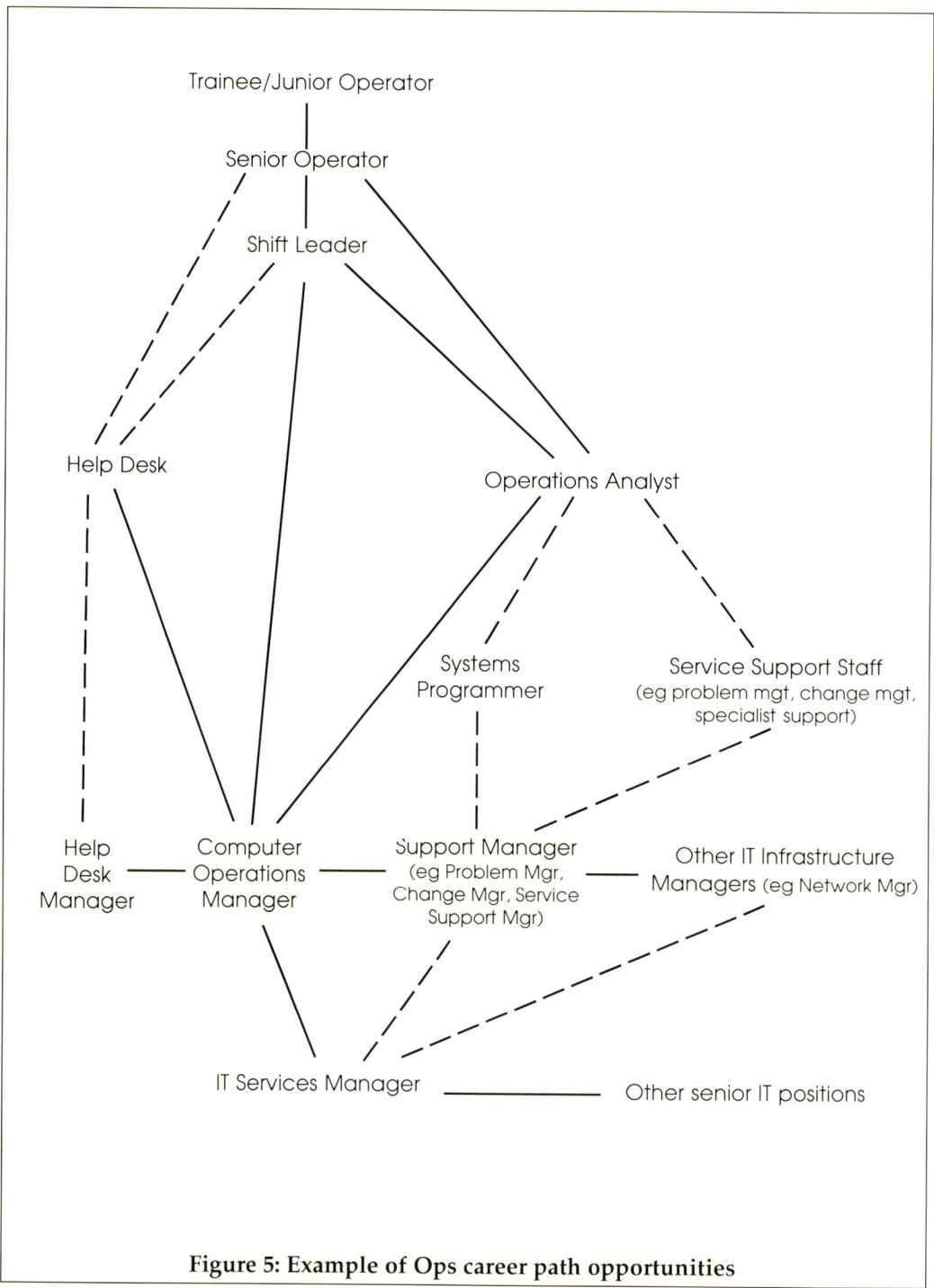

Figure 5: Example of Ops career path opportunities

Section 3
Planning for computer operations management

Figure 6: Organizational Structure

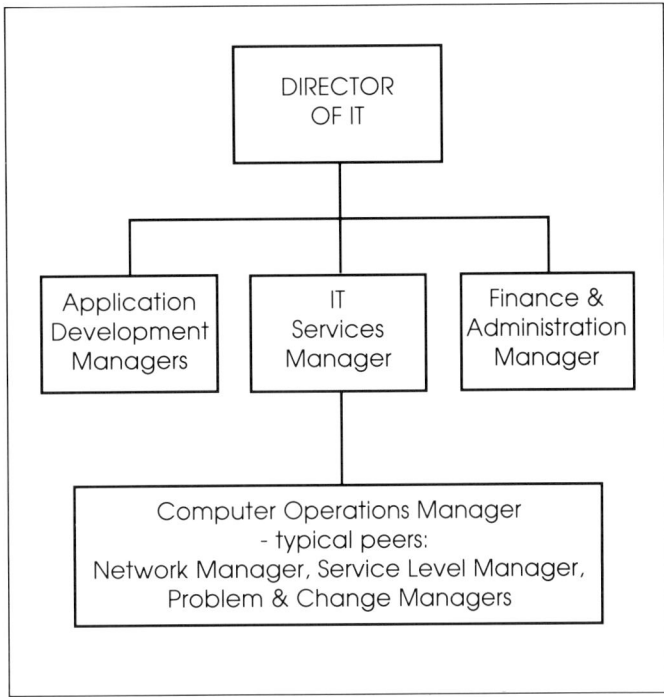

Figure 6 shows how the Ops Manager fits into a typical IT Directorate structure.

This organization reflects the fact that IT services management, which includes the provision of service for applications development management, is one of the key functions of the IT Directorate. The IT Services Manager has a key responsibility within his or her peer group to ensure that the IT 'product' that reaches the user is of the appropriate quality.

3.3.2.2 The Operations organization

Figure 7, overleaf, shows the Ops organization within IT Services. Operations analysts are shown as part of the Ops area, although they appear as part of the support function in some organizations. In either case the reporting line is not critical and can be used to balance the numeric make-up of reporting structures. What is critical is that the roles are clearly defined and understood whatever reporting structure is chosen.

The Ops structure shown here gives a sound organization to meet operational targets.

79

The IT Infrastructure Library
Computer Operations Management

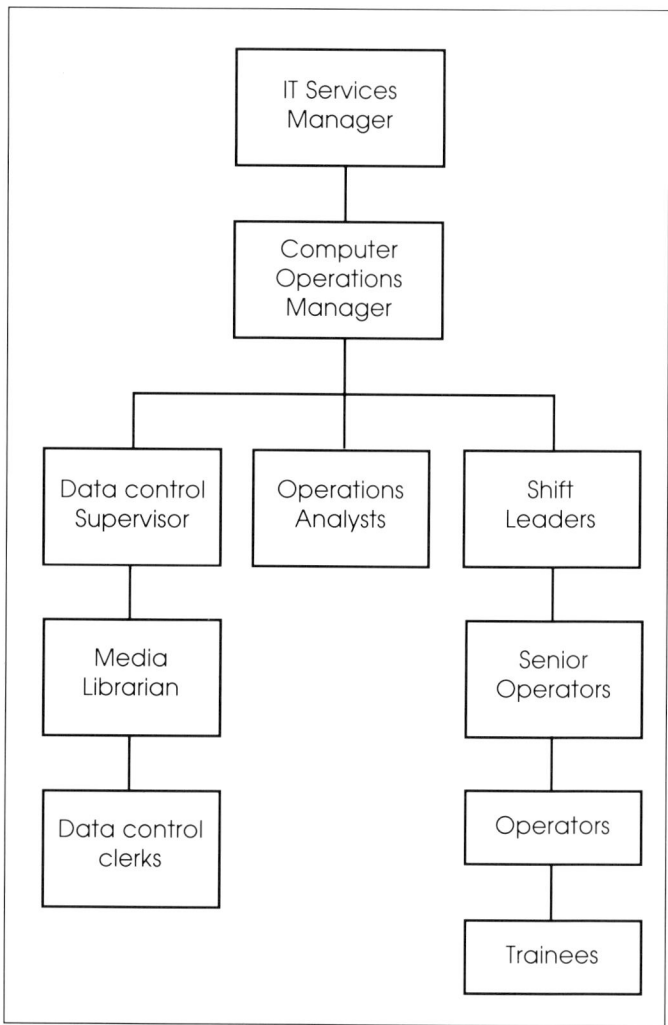

Figure 7: Operations Structure

3.3.2.3 Operations shift patterns

For Government departments the Civil Service Pay and Conditions of Service apply, and there are clearly defined rules for shift operations. However, organizations may find the following generic guidance of use.

The need to maximize the efficient usage of expensive IT equipment means that most Ops areas work on a shift basis. The structure of the shifts can depend on a number of factors:

* the business service requirement

Section 3
Planning for computer operations management

* the power/capacity of the computers
* the number of staff
* the volume and structure of work
* personnel issues (trades union agreements, local social custom, etc).

Senior IT management is responsible for deciding, in broad terms, the operational hours and shift-working patterns needed to satisfy organizations' business needs in a cost-effective way. Ops should arrive at the best arrangements for the business, and for staff, within senior management's guidelines. For example, Ops management should ensure that obvious business peaks are unaffected by shift changes; eg if your online day start up is 08.00, your shift change should not be at the same time!

For all shift patterns a half hour changeover period is a good idea, both to encourage good shift relations and to ensure effective communication of key processing issues.

2-shift working

This is the normal pattern to cover an online service during normal office hours and a mainly batch workload during the evening. Usual shift times are 07.00 - 15.30 and 15.00 - 23.30.

This shift pattern is often used to give staff a split week of say three days and two evenings and then three evenings and two days. This pattern helps minimize disruption of operators' social lives.

3-shift working

A third shift fills the night hours of 23.00 - 07.30, normally to accommodate batch and housekeeping work. The night shift generally works either four or five nights a week dependent on workload. It is not advisable to split night working spells over different weeks because it would disturb staff sleep patterns. If five nights are worked, the fifth can be Friday, or Sunday, night dependent on local requirements. Instead of a fifth night, some organizations work a Saturday daytime shift.

4-shift working

This arrangement is generally used where seven days-per-week, 24 hours-a-day operation is needed. The shift patterns are normally worked out on a monthly cycle basis with considerable local variation. The major consideration is to ensure consistent coverage whilst allowing staff some order to their social lives. Each shift, for example, would work one weekend per month and one week of nights, but the week of days/evenings and the full week of nights can be manipulated and are usually worked out locally by arrangement.

12-hour shift patterns

12-hour shifts are, or have been, used in a number of sites. Whilst they can be very welcome for Ops staff (working only three days per week) they can be disruptive to the running of effective Ops in a number of ways.

During the last four hours of a shift, particularly a night shift, operators can be especially prone to error due to tiredness, which can be of major concern particularly if the errors occur in the early morning, at online start-up time.

There is often a long gap between the end of a cycle of shifts and the start of the next. Invariably something may have changed in the intervening period. There is a real danger that, unless a very meticulous handover and briefing is held at the start of a new cycle, and a good inter-shift communications system is in place, the newly-arrived shift will not know about the change.

Holidays are difficult to administer (eg is a 12-hour shift a day or a day and a half?); and any sickness or absence is significant.

This shift pattern is now in diminishing use.

Shift payments

A payment is usually made to staff that work a shift pattern to compensate for the unsocial hours worked. The level is dependent on local arrangements and the hours worked, being either a lump sum per period, or a percentage of salary. Some typical ranges:

* 2 shifts 10 - 15 % of salary

* 3 shifts 15 - 20 %

* 4 shifts 15 - 30 % depending on pattern agreed.

Shift payments are not usually part of base salary and are not paid when shifts are not worked. This reduction in pay can cause career and financial problems when a move off shift is necessary. These problems can be overcome if the move off shifts is to take up a post on promotion, with the extra pay offsetting part or all of the loss. Alternatively a discretionary diminishing 'coming-off-shift allowance' can be paid as an incentive during say a 6 or 12 month period. At the end of this period, salary has normally advanced and the difference is not felt so severely.

3.3.3 Training

Training is crucial to the ongoing effectiveness of Ops. The training of staff is a key responsibility of the Ops Manager, and should not be neglected.

Section 3
Planning for computer operations management

3.3.3.1 Training plans

Each member of staff should have an individual, staged, training plan. This plan has two principal objectives:

* to ensure that staff perform their assigned role within the limits of their ability
* to develop staff to perform tasks in the future, either in their current role or in a new assignment.

To formulate the staff training plan, all staff members should be counselled by their direct supervisor, possibly as part of the appraisal process. This counselling session must:

* establish and agree the individual's areas of weakness in the current role
* identify additional areas where improved skills and knowledge would help to improve performance
* project likely changes in role due to a career or organization-influenced move and any new skills required
* identify potential training events, reading or hands-on guidance that would address these points
* jointly agree a training plan that stretches for a minimum period of one year; in many cases planning can extend out to two or three years or longer
* agree any action required by either the member of staff or supervisor to put the plan into action.

The training plan should be monitored by the supervisor on a regular basis to ensure the benefit is being felt in the staff performance and to check that the training received has been applied.

3.3.3.2 Likely training requirements

For Ops staff there could be a wide range of training required, some potentially applicable to all staff, some in purely specialist areas. Topics relevant to all staff include:

* induction
* IT service management
* business appreciation
* communication (written and verbal) skills

* time management
* team leading and management of staff
* Ops planning and control
* basic principles of computer operations

and, for specialist areas:

* data control and librarian techniques
* computer operating
* operating systems and utilities
* networking basics.

3.3.3.3 Types of training available

There are currently many different methods of training available. Which are chosen depends on:

* the individual concerned
* the topic being taught
* the time and money available.

Hands-on
This is an excellent way for trainees to gain specific experience onsite and for them to learn to operate equipment without having had formal (eg manufacturer's) training. It is important that trainees are closely supervised in the early stages of hands-on training, particularly when using electrical or mechanical devices. Later, when the trainee is more experienced, more unsupervised work, but checked at regular intervals, is suggested.

Reading
The reading of background information or programmed text can provide useful training, particularly if combined with practical sessions or frequent testing.

Internal courses
The range of internal courses can vary from induction for newcomers through to business appreciation and management. This option can often be the best and most cost-effective for learning people-skills. Consult carefully with your training centre to determine course suitability before selecting a specific course.

External courses
These are particularly applicable to IT service management and operating skills, where inhouse training might not be cost-effective owing to lack of numbers.

Section 3
Planning for computer operations management

Computer-based or interactive video courses
These are useful for most training needs when time is at a premium. They can be used onsite over a period to save losing staff for two to five days or more. These courses are particularly good for technically-based skills.

Projects
These can provide a useful opportunity for Ops staff to develop and stretch their abilities. For example the installation of a new bank of disks could be project-managed by a Shift Leader (under the watchful eye of a more experienced member of staff), as a way of building the Shift Leader's interpersonal, planning and project management skills.

Whichever method of training is selected, every opportunity should be given for the individual to put the learning into practice. Training must not be treated as a 'perk' for staff. It is an intrinsic part of their working year and must be linked by the training plan to both their work and their future development.

3.4 Timing

In a greenfield site it is appropriate to plan the Ops function before computer equipment is installed.

For all sites, Ops' responsibilities and procedures must be planned prior to the commencement of an operational service. In general there should be a lead time of up to 3 months between introducing Ops procedures and taking on operational work, to give the procedures time to become established. This lead time would allow for the writing of all the procedures mentioned within this module and the testing of the procedures for suitability and accuracy. Once a procedure is written, the procedure should be used, where possible, by a selection of staff to find out if the procedure is correct and easy to use. The staff should report back on the procedure and any necessary changes should be made.

A similar lead time is necessary between delivery and installation of major system hardware and software and introduction of an operational service (unless the hardware and software is very similar to existing hardware and software). This lead time gives the site time to thoroughly test that the IT system is ready to provide the operational service. This testing can usually be accomplished through the running of application acceptance testing or by using test programs designed for site trials in advance of the 'live' date. Government organizations using CCTA's procurement service should use the CCTA rules for tendering and general conditions of contract, CC88.

Subsequent hardware and software changes should be subject to normal change management procedures.

Ops staff should be in place before operational service starts but the filling of posts can be staged progressively. The Ops Manager should be in place around 6 months in advance, but a trainee operator need only arrive at least 1 week prior to operational service.

Section 4
Implementation

4. Implementation

4.1 Procedures

The implementation phase for the procedures planned as described in section 3 involves:

* informing all Ops and other relevant IT and user staff and managers the date from which the new procedures come into effect (4.1.1)

* ensuring that everyone is adequately trained in the new procedures and is clear on how they are affected (4.1.1)

* installing and implementing hardware and software tools (4.1.2)

* testing Ops procedures (4.1.3)

* implementing budgetary controls (4.1.4)

* supporting affected users and Ops and other IT staff to help ensure a smooth implementation (4.1.5)

* finalizing arrangements for out-of-hours working (4.1.6)

* putting the procedures into effect (4.1.7)

* putting right any deficiencies (4.1.8)

* ensuring everyone concerned adheres to procedures (4.1.9).

It is important to use project management techniques when implementing any new process. PRINCE is the CCTA-recommended method for project management.

4.1.1 Informing staff and users

All Ops staff, other IT staff, and many users will be affected by the implementation of the new procedures. The Ops Manager must ensure that everyone knows when the new procedures are to take effect, and how they will be affected. The Ops Manager should ensure that all of the procedures are communicated to relevant managers and participants.

The IT Infrastructure Library
Computer Operations Management

To determine who is likely to need what information, track the various Ops processes through and decide who are the interested parties. For example, interested parties when setting up and implementing applications acceptance procedures are likely to be:

* operations analysts
* problem management and specialist support
* Help Desk
* applications development management
* user managers
* shift operators.

The interested parties and their managers should receive an explanatory overview of the processes, a draft of the procedures for review and constructive comment, and a final copy of the completed procedures when they are ready. This collaborative approach should lead to acceptance of, and commitment to, Ops processes when they go live.

Ops staff and any other affected IT staff must be fully trained in the new procedures before a live service starts. For sites adopting the new procedures at a time that coincides with the installation of new computer(s), final hands-on training of some staff can take place during acceptance trials and the subsequent run-up period to live operations. There must however be enough trained staff to operate the computer(s) competently during acceptance trials and in the run-up to live operations.

4.1.2 Install and implement hardware and software tools

Required hardware and software tools must be installed, tested and implemented in parallel with the development and testing of Ops procedures (see 4.1.3).

There are lead-times for the supply of hardware and software tools. Length of the lead time depends upon a number of factors including whether the software is bespoke, or available off-the-shelf.

Feasibility studies should have been run to decide which tools are the best for the site and the computer environment. Once the tools have been selected, the organization needs to decide the level of help it needs from the tool suppliers to implement the tools.

Section 4
Implementation

Contracts should be used as a basis for the supply of tools and acceptance testing must be carried out on the tools once delivered and installed. Some tools, because of their complexity and the high level of change they cause at the site, should have a phased implementation.

All staff who use the tools must be suitably trained.

4.1.3 Test Ops procedures

As Ops procedures are developed, their effectiveness and practicability should be tested: the procedures should be tested individually and also together as a sequence of dependent procedures. Sections outside Ops may be involved in the testing particularly when the sections are affected by the new procedures.

If the site is a greenfield one or one that is installing a computer system of a type that is new to it, the opportunity can be taken to do final testing of procedures during equipment trials and during the period before go-live.

Any problems remaining when the Ops function commences operation must be fed into the IT infrastructure problem management system (ie the problem management system for live operations) and resolved at source in accordance with their severity.

4.1.4 Implement budgetary control

The budgetary controls planned previously (3.1.4.4) must be implemented with the help of the IT Cost Manager. The Ops Manager must be clear from the outset about the scope of the post's budgetary responsibility.

The Ops Manager should develop internal checks or controls on costs that complement the overall IT cost control. The following are examples of cost-control checks:

* media librarian to report monthly on media used, current stock levels and likely future requirements, also on media allocated during the period and reason(s)

* shift leaders to report on paper or printlines used during a weekly or monthly period to establish trends in paper usage.

Likely expenditure into the future should be gauged - capacity planning activity and SLA reviews provide information to complement the projections based on current trends.

The IT Infrastructure Library
Computer Operations Management

To ensure that money is spent only on approved items (eg purchasing particular types of tape and stationery) it is recommended that the Ops Manager personally takes responsibility for signing all purchase orders.

The Ops Manager should retain information on the amount, and cost, of any overtime worked and the reason for working it, and may wish to be personally responsible for authorizing overtime.

To help reduce the cost of operations, operability and acceptance standards must be implemented for all forthcoming projects from their date of inception. Recently-commenced projects can also have the standards applied. Consideration should be given to a programme of retrospective implementation.

4.1.5 Support affected staff

Organizations should ensure that all staff and any users affected by the introduction of the new procedures are adequately supported. Technical support personnel should be available for consultation by Ops and the Help Desk as appropriate.

4.1.6 Finalize arrangements for out-of-hours working

Arrangements for out-of-hours working must be finalized. Staff conditions and welfare matters associated with out-of-hours callout and support should be settled. The support groups' management and also personnel management should be involved to ensure these matters are dealt with practically and reasonably.

4.1.7 Put the procedures into effect

Provided that the procedures have been adequately tested, and information has been circulated sufficiently, all that should be necessary to implement new procedures is to announce their start date and begin using them.

4.1.8 Cope with implementation problems

In the event of something going seriously wrong with implementation, all staff must be aware of the course of action to be taken, and the effect it has on them. It is likely that things can, in time, be put right.

Section 4
Implementation

Faulty procedures should have shown up in testing, but, given time, can be put right. If training is inadequate that can be put right. If the equipment performance is inadequate that should have showed up in testing but it can be put right, perhaps at the vendor's expense depending on contractual conditions.

If, as recommended, a gap has been allowed before critical live operations begin, extra efforts should be made to rectify the worst problems in time. In extremis, you may have to invoke a contingency plan but that will not help where procedures or training have proved inadequate.

Some types of less serious implementation problem can be left unresolved at the start of live operations in accordance with the normal rules of change and problem management. Information on these problems must be transferred to the IT infrastructure problem management system for late resolution according to problem severity.

4.1.9 Ensure adherence to procedures

During and immediately following implementation, efforts must be made to ensure Ops staff and others adhere strictly to the new procedures. For example, the Ops manual should require that operators record all significant operational events. It helps to have a checklist for each of the shift leaders to detail exactly the checkpoints they are expected to meet or record. Management should deal supportively but firmly with non-adherence to laid-down procedures. It is easier to correct problem practices early on before they become entrenched.

4.2 Dependencies

To implement an Ops function successfully the following must be met:

* procedures sufficiently ready
* staff training sufficiently well advanced
* users trained
* all required hardware and software tools accepted and working satisfactorily
* accommodation and environment accepted and functioning satisfactorily

The IT Infrastructure Library
Computer Operations Management

* budgetary controls in place
* operability standards in place
* all out-of-hours arrangements documented
* all personnel issues resolved.

4.3 Staff

The staff described in 3.3 assume their full Ops responsibilities at implementation time.

4.4 Timing

The introduction of the procedures described in 4.1 should be carried out to a timetable set by the Project Management or Change Advisory Board.

Section 5
Post-implementation and audit

5. Post-implementation and audit

A post-implementation review must be carried out soon after implementation of the Ops function (5.1.1).

The ongoing operation of the Ops function is based on the plans described in 3.1.

The Ops Manager, being the key player in the successful functioning of Ops, should be subject to regular performance reviews (5.1.2).

The Ops function must be reviewed regularly for efficiency/effectiveness (5.1.3) and audited for compliance to laid-down procedures (5.1.5). Deficiencies must be put right at source.

The regular reviews should look forward and plans must be made to ensure that Ops continues to provide quality services in the face of changing user needs and business requirements.

In some circumstances, a review of the Ops function by external consultants may be beneficial (5.1.6).

5.1 Procedures

5.1.1 Post-implementation review

Some 2 to 3 months after implementation of the Ops function, a post-implementation review should be carried out, to check:

* whether the Ops function was implemented and is working as planned - if not, is it better than planned or must corrective action be instigated to bring it up to the required standard?

* whether changes need to be made to the planning process itself to prevent a recurrence of planning problems

* whether the required quality of IT service is being delivered and expected benefits, are being realized (see, for example, 3.1.10) and, if not, what if anything can be done to bring them about.

Any deficiencies must be diagnosed and put right at source.

The IT Infrastructure Library
Computer Operations Management

5.1.2 The Operations Manager - performance reviews

The Ops Manager's performance must regularly be reviewed against the job's agreed targets and objectives. The Ops Manager has a critical influence on the Ops function and any degradation in performance must rapidly be reversed. Whoever or whatever is at fault should be identified and the fault put right.

5.1.3 Efficiency and effectiveness reviews and management checks

Regular reviews, at least every 6 months, must be carried out by IT Services management to check that Ops is functioning efficiently and effectively. These reviews should look forward, and plans must be made or updated to cope with future changes in IT infrastructure and usage. For the reviews of Ops' planning, IT workload and capacity plans must be examined to get a clear picture of the services that Ops will be required to provide over say the next 18-24 months. The IT Services Manager and the Service Level Manager must be involved in these reviews and must ultimately approve, modify or reject the plans.

The Ops Manager must **continually** review the Ops function, and must ensure that necessary management checks are built into the day-to-day functioning of Ops.

Each review should compare the quality of Ops with that of the previous period(s) and should check that adequate progress is made in carrying out plans and putting right problems identified in previous reviews.

The efficiency and effectiveness reviews of Ops must consider the following items:

* IT service provision (5.1.3.1; also 3.1.10)
* relationships with other IT teams (5.1.3 2)
* use of other IT infrastructure management systems (5.1.3.3)
* care of hardware and the environment (5.1.3.4 and 3.1.10)
* computer room housekeeping (5.1.3.5)
* adherence to budgets (5.1.3.6)

- Ops staff are adequately trained (3.3)
- staff morale levels (3.3)
- the Ops copy of the contingency plan is up to date and Ops staff are aware of their responsibilities (3.1.4.5).

Ops staff should be encouraged to comment on the processes and systems being used, and to voice any concerns. These should be evaluated, and improvements or solutions applied as appropriate.

5.1.3.1 IT service provision

The main indicator of Ops' effectiveness in providing IT services is that Ops successfully contributes to the meeting of SLAs. To get information on how well Ops is achieving this, the service that Ops provides in support of SLAs should be reviewed formally with the Service Level Manager at least monthly. Any problems in meeting service levels should be identified and corrected via the problem management system but it is helpful to carry out these regular formal reviews to ensure that problems are not missed and that opportunities for improvement are identified and acted upon.

The following questions should be answered for feeding into the IT Services management reviews of Ops:

- are the targets for availability of online systems being met?
- are reports being despatched correctly and promptly?
- are operational problems putting these or other service criteria at risk?
- is Ops dealing with incidents effectively?
- are backup/recovery plans tested and adequate?

Data is fed into the reviews of IT service provision from various sources:

- the problem management system
- the change management system
- Ops staff and Ops logs
- the monitoring of SLAs.

The IT Infrastructure Library
Computer Operations Management

5.1.3.2 Relations with other IT teams

It is vital that good working relationships are maintained with other parts of the IT Directorate. The opportunity should be available at regular (say, monthly) IT management meetings to identify and resolve any relationship problems. Trends must be reviewed at the efficiency/effectiveness review meetings, and any worsening of relations must be diagnosed at source and put right.

Ops must collaborate in reviews by IT Services management of adherence by others to systems that Ops set up, eg operability standards.

5.1.3.3 Use of other IT infrastructure management systems

Ops must regularly review the systems it uses that are someone else's responsibility, eg problem management system, and must report back to the manager concerned any problems or opportunities for improvement. Trends must be reviewed at the regular efficiency/effectiveness review meetings and any problems must be diagnosed at source and put right.

5.1.3.4 Hardware and environment

The maintenance of the hardware and computer-room environment is essential if IT service quality is to be maintained. There should be checks in a number of areas. At the regular efficiency/effectiveness reviews, trends and statistics on the activities and services described below must be tabled and any problems diagnosed, and identified for correction at source. All required changes must be reviewed at the next meeting to check that they have been carried out.

Hardware

There should be regular meetings with the site engineer(s), typically monthly, to ensure that maintenance schedules are being adhered to and that incidents are being handled satisfactorily. These meetings provide an opportunity to discuss forthcoming changes that may have an impact on service provision. (All changes must be controlled by the change management system. Processor upgrades in particular should be planned early and notified to the change management system well in advance).

Section 5
Post-implementation and audit

The shift leader should check, at least weekly, that the peripheral cleaning schedules are being followed. Peripheral cleaning standards should conform to manufacturers' guidelines and be documented in the appropriate equipment manual. Typically, tape units and impact printers require cleaning daily or per shift in heavy usage.

Environment

Electrical supply and air conditioning should be checked regularly. The electrical supply voltages are checked on the Power Distribution Units to verify that they are within limits. This checking may be done by a maintenance engineer. For the air conditioning the temperature and humidity levels are checked. There is usually a chart showing these levels in the computer room. The chart should be changed regularly and old charts retained as necessary.

Computer room cleaning should be carried out on a daily basis to avoid excessive build up of dust. Cleaners should not be allowed to touch equipment. An underfloor clean should be performed every 6 months.

Other checks that should be carried out include:

* regular testing of any fire detection and suppression equipment
* regular testing of water detection equipment
* regular fire drills for all Ops staff
* maintenance schedules for non-computer equipment; eg tape cleaners, offline equipment.

Security

Security checks should be undertaken on a random basis to ensure that security procedures work, and are being followed. These checks should include:

* a review of access logs to check that only authorized staff have entered
* a review of overnight media access to ensure there is no unauthorized use of media
* a check of the magnetic media to ensure that none are missing
* a check of numbered cheques or special stationery
* attempts to access as an intruder to check that physical access restrictions work

* a discussion with the security section to determine its view of computer room security.

These checks should be carried out by a senior member of the Ops staff.

5.1.3.5 Computer room housekeeping

Users, management and other visitors will often judge Ops by the appearance of the computer room. The cleanliness and orderliness and its employees' work habits can make a lasting, good or bad, impression. The Ops Manager should ensure that the impression is positive. In addition the appearance of the computer room can influence the effectiveness and efficiency of staff performance, and an untidy computer room could fail to comply with health and safety requirements.

The following checklist can be used to evaluate housekeeping standards in the computer room:

* surplus or broken furniture present
* excessive number of tapes/cartridges not racked
* printout or cards scattered at random
* excessive number of operator and/or maintenance manuals not stored in the proper place
* newspapers and magazines at the control console
* surplus disconnected equipment
* extra floor panels or floor panels not in place and nobody working on installation
* equipment unserviceable for an excessive period
* fire drill and any relevant safety information not posted or not current
* smoking, eating or drinking
* secure areas not secured
* equipment or supplies in access ways
* spare parts not properly stored
* equipment covers not on equipment
* printers in use with covers up.

Section 5
Post-implementation and audit

Statistics and trends on these items should be tabled at the regular reviews of Ops carried out by IT Services management.

The above standards can be enforced in a variety of ways such as the development of periodic action plans to be carried out by nominated Ops teams or the incorporation of the standards into shift handover procedures. Organizations must ensure that vendor and environment engineers play their part and that it is not all left up to the Ops staff to maintain standards. The Ops Manager should supply engineers with the computer room rules and should clearly indicate where they are expected to comply.

The Ops Manager can sometimes alleviate housekeeping problems for Ops staff by contracting out services such as cleaning.

Improving computer room housekeeping practices can have a significant effect on productivity, employee morale and the image of Ops within the organization. For any improvement effort to succeed the IT Services Manager and the Ops Manager must fully support and encourage it and carry out appropriate checks to ensure its ongoing positive effects.

5.1.3.6 Budget and consumables

The consumption levels of consumables such as paper, tapes, cartridges, and printer ribbons must be recorded. These consumption levels directly affect the budget, and any increase over forecast should be investigated, the forecast should be corrected, and the forecasting method improved.

A record should be kept of each month's Ops expenditure, and returns should be submitted to the IT Cost Manager at agreed intervals. Significant variances to forecast should be discussed to determine why they occurred. If valid, they may require either an increase in budget or an adjustment later in the year. In such cases, a way of improving the forecasting method should be sought. The budget should never be allowed to get out of control as remedial action is often difficult or impossible.

Future budgetary requirements depend on future IT usage, plans for which are available to Ops via SLA reviews, capacity plans, and IT tactical plans.

The IT Infrastructure Library
Computer Operations Management

Summarized reports of Ops' expenditure against budget must be presented to the regular reviews by IT Services management of Ops, for planning and control purposes.

5.1.4 User involvement in reviewing Ops

It is recommended that users are regularly given information on Ops' performance, and an opportunity to make their views about Ops' performance known, for any necessary action by IT management.

This user involvement can be achieved by inviting selected user representatives to participate in the regular reviews by IT services management of Ops' efficiency and effectiveness. Alternatively, Ops' efficiency and effectiveness can be discussed at the regular reviews of Service Level Agreements to which users are a party.

Before the meetings, Ops should distribute to the attendees what they believe their performance to have been in meeting Service Level Requirements during the period concerned. Commentary on any Ops' deficiencies must be included. The reason for any deviations from SLAs must be identified and actions agreed at the meetings to prevent a recurrence.

5.1.5 Audits

Audits are carried out to:

* check for compliance to procedures
* make recommendations for improvements to the procedures.

Audits should be conducted by IT staff independent of Ops fairly regularly (every 6 to 12 months; consider doing some unannounced!) and consideration should be given to an annual audit by external auditors.

Typically these audits check items such as the following:

* that the online service is started at the correct times
* that batch jobs are run at correct times
* that prints are produced in accordance with schedules
* the number of incidents, interrupting IT service provision, that are caused by Ops and the extent to which procedures could be improved to prevent recurrence

Section 5
Post-implementation and audit

* that the number of such incidents is decreasing or increasing - if increasing what steps is the Ops Manager taking to improve matters?

* how quickly the Ops domain incidents are notified to the problem management system, and directly to the Help Desk and Network Control

* that Ops domain incidents are escalated for further investigation or management attention within the required timeframe

* that users who contact Ops directly are told politely but firmly to use the Help Desk

* that Ops changes, agreed by the Change Manager, are put into effect as authorized and within the required timeframe

* that Ops procedural documentation is up to date

* that records that Ops should keep (eg peripheral maintenance, media usage, shift incident logs) are kept correctly

* that maintenance is being carried out as laid-down, or is there evidence of corner cutting?

* that standards of security are being adhered to

* that health and safety standards are being complied with

* that expenditure is being contained within budget

* that Ops' plans are clearly documented and cover the required forward window

* that Ops staff training is carried out in accordance with training plans and that training records are up-to-date.

In addition, many of the items covered in section 5.1.3 can be used as audit-checklist items.

Audits are essential to give IT management confidence that the required quality of service will be maintained. Auditors must be given every cooperation.

To ensure there is minimal disruption to the day-to-day production, there should be a pre-audit planning session with the auditors to establish a structured programme for the audit. A senior member of Ops staff should be assigned to the auditors as a liaison point.

Audit reports must be agreed by Ops management, and tabled to IT Services management for agreement on any necessary follow-up actions. Subsequent audits must check that follow-up actions have been carried out.

5.1.6 External consultant reviews

It can be productive to employ external consultants to get an independent assessment of the quality of Ops and of Ops activities where there is known to be room for improvement. Invariably other aspects of IT service provision also have to be reviewed.

Likely issues to be addressed are:

* if IT service costs are increasing as a proportion of overall organizational running costs, are the IT service costs acceptable, or could they be reduced by

    - better or different work practices, eg more automated Ops

    - changes to the organizational structure, eg introduction of a Bridge

    - changes to part of the IT configuration or layout

    - adjustment of staffing levels

    - better management reporting

* the adequacy of staff career training and development

* the reasons why Ops consistently cause SLA targets to be missed (if they do)

* breaches in security

* whether the IT service, or the Ops part of it, could be better or more economically provided by an outside organization.

It is important that any findings are agreed by the staff and management in Ops and other IT Services teams, and that all necessary follow-up action is taken. Subsequent management reviews of Ops should review progress on these follow-up actions.

Section 5
Post-implementation and audit

5.2 Dependencies

Ops must organize itself to cope with changing business needs and to exploit changing technology. IT services are constantly changing due to the needs of organizations' businesses. These businesses generate demands for new hardware capacity and new applications that all have to be processed. Ops runs hardware and applications that have to change to meet business needs. Ops generates requests for new hardware to make Ops more efficient (in collaboration with capacity management).

It is especially important to keep Ops' use of support tools and automation aids under review - new ways of working and further automation may be feasible and cost-justifiable. The dependencies for successful Ops described in 3.2 must be kept under review.

5.3 Staff

Staff are an important resource and must feel part of the decision making process. This feeling of involvement affects their work and performance. Therefore, communication through all levels of Ops is vital.

Meetings of all the staff employed in Ops should be held at least quarterly with meetings of smaller groups, eg individual shifts, being held monthly. If shift workers have trouble attending, consideration should be given to holding the meetings in conjunction with a social event.

In addition to holding regular staff meetings, Ops management should consider issuing staff bulletins, eg on notice boards. This method of disseminating information should be used, in conjunction with shift notices, to inform staff of day-to-day operational issues.

Shift leaders have an important role to play in disseminating information to shift staff. It must be a clear responsibility of the shift leader to keep shift staff informed of all relevant information that may affect them - for example organization-wide and IT Directorate news, technology updates (general and specific to the site), changes pending and implemented.

5.3.1 Organization

The organization of Ops should be reviewed in line with management's objectives. Staff should be consulted regarding any changes and their input requested as part of the decision-making process.

When organizational changes are required, they should be discussed with the affected individuals and sections; explain why they are being made and what effect they will have on staff. This discussion helps to avoid any unnecessary dissent and win staff commitment.

5.3.2 Management of staff

There are a number of key issues concerning the management of staff. Like all staff, Ops staff require management effort to ensure they perform as required.

Training

It is important that the plans outlined in section 3.3.3 are reviewed at least annually with each member of staff to ensure:

* that management checks that training has been satisfactorily undertaken

* that the training plans are updated to reflect any new training requirements identified.

Comfort

Issues such as rest rooms, coffee machines, desks, health and safety should occasionally be reviewed to ensure that staff are working in a clean and pleasant environment. This effort is normally repaid in higher productivity and fewer complaints about working conditions.

Retention, motivation and appraisal

The turnover of Ops staff can be high. To help avoid this problem, it is important to keep motivation and team spirit high, which can be done in a number of ways:

* maintaining job interest through allocating projects to staff at all levels - minor projects for more junior staff to some quite complex ones for more experienced staff such as shift leaders

* keeping staff well informed of changes in the IT Directorate and in the organization as a whole; this encourages interest in the broad picture

* organizing regular social events, perhaps to celebrate good performance in meeting production targets consistently

* encouraging staff at all levels to attend special interest seminars, lectures and other 'industry forum' events, attendance at which can both educate and motivate for nominal cost

Section 5
Post-implementation and audit

* encouraging a degree of competition between shifts (if they are evenly balanced in terms of ability), by publishing the month's overnight performance in terms of hitting the critical path targets

* regularly conducting job appraisals, against agreed job targets and objectives, to confirm good performance and enable any problems to be worked at jointly, thus avoiding the need for 'crisis' interviews to tackle poor performance.

Shift patterns These should be reviewed at least annually to confirm that they are both meeting business targets and are not having an unnecessarily severe impact on operators' home lives. Any changes should be considered in consultation with IT management and the shift staff concerned.

5.4 Timing

A post-implementation review should be carried out within 3 months of implementing an Ops function.

When Ops is running live production systems, the efficiency and effectiveness reviews and audits indicated in 5.1 should be carried out at the frequencies shown, eg:

* IT services management reviews of Ops' efficiency and effectiveness - every 6 months

* service level reviews with the Service Level Manager - monthly

* relations with other IT teams (at IT management meetings) - monthly

* reviews of hardware engineers' performance - monthly

* internal audits - every 6 to 12 months

* external audits - every 12 months

* external/consultant reviews - as and when required.

These audits and reviews can be used constructively to reappraise and enhance performance by implementing the agreed recommendations rapidly. If the Ops area is allowed to run without frequent internal efficiency and effectiveness reviews and audits, it can rapidly become complacent.

The IT Infrastructure Library
Computer Operations Management

Section 6
Benefits, costs and possible problems

6. Benefits, costs and possible problems

6.1 Benefits

This module creates a framework for Ops to interrelate with other aspects of IT service provision as covered in other IT Infrastructure Library modules. This framework ensures that the role of Ops is clear both to itself and to other parts of the organization. The module helps organizations that wish to develop or improve the professionalism of their operations practices. Specific benefits that can be expected from using the guidance in the module include:

* a framework for cost management and cost reduction
* help with the provision and maintenance of quality IT services
* clear definition of the roles and responsibilities of individuals within operations, which
  - is good for staff morale
  - makes recruitment easier
  - makes a systematic approach to the assessment of staff performance and promotability easier
* a platform for the development of automation in Ops and the use of an Ops Bridge (which offers productivity and service quality improvements)
* quicker solutions to incidents and problems, with clear definition of responsibilities - this in turn gives rise to improvements in availability and avoids problem recurrences
* a structure that helps ensure harmonious relationships with suppliers
* a climate within which procedures are accepted as being the norm so that reliance on individual inherited skills diminishes
* generation of a professional environment where the performance of everybody can rise to the level of the best.

6.2 Costs

The main costs incurred in adopting the guidance in this module are likely to be:

* cost and time of adopting, tailoring and producing the procedures described in the module
* cost of any new software packages required
* cost of any additional equipment required, eg data cartridge devices and the data cartridges.

However, the development of Ops' professionalism is an investment which in the long run pays for itself both with automation, which reduces cost and improves quality, and with moves away from a dependence on inherited skills and local undocumented knowledge.

6.3 Possible problems

In most organizations the professional practices described in this module are seen as the obviously correct way to operate. There may, however, be some resistance to changes in working practices. Ops staff have traditionally relied on historical knowledge and often see themselves as central to the efficient running of the organization (they are indeed very important). The trend towards systematic procedures with more clearly defined roles and responsibilities, and above all the move towards automation are, however, eliminating the 'craft' tradition.

In this climate, changes to bring Ops working practices into line with the guidance in this module cannot necessarily be introduced rapidly. These changes should be handled as far as possible by the existing operations staff to ensure committed knowledgeable change, at measured pace, to modern professional practices.

To avoid staff morale problems and to ensure staff take ownership of changes, it is recommended that any consultancy bought in to modernize practices is used in support of the people onsite rather than in place of them. This approach will reduce the risks and the costs of achieving professionalism.

Many organizations use the argument that "we are too busy fighting the fire to build a new house". However, it must be realized that if things are to get better, at some time the organization needs to take decisive action. In general, the more the fire-fighting activity, the greater the need for radical change.

Section 7
Tools

7. Tools

This section contains guidance and checklists of items to consider for the different types of software tools likely to be required by Ops. Specifics to check for are listed under the individual types of tools. However, some checks are applicable to all Ops tools. These checks include:

* how much is the total cost of the package?
* is the package compatible with the operating system and other packages in use at the organization?
* is the package easy to use?
* are the management reports produced adequate?
* what vendor support is provided?

As the scope and number of Ops tools is vast and the market very volatile, specific examples of available packages are not cited. Ops Managers need to keep in contact with software providers and to read the appropriate trade press to ensure they keep abreast of relevant developments.

7.1 Schedulers

What they do

Scheduling packages are now widely used, especially in larger sites. They are used for a number of reasons, in particular to:

* automate the scheduling of work, and help in automated operations
* reduce schedule idle-times and identify bottlenecks
* ensure consistency and efficiency of schedules
* ensure centralized control of scheduling (if required).

What to look for

Knowing the critical path of all the jobs is useful when setting up the scheduling package. The critical path shows the most important jobs, with regard to scheduling, running on any day.

The scheduling package should normally be set up to run the jobs according to the date. It should know which jobs need to run on which date. The date also triggers weekly and monthly schedules (for example, on every Friday certain jobs are triggered to run).

The package should also run on time and dependency criteria. For example a job can be set up to run every day at 9.00 am, or to run when other jobs have finished, or data files are available, which can mean that some jobs run sooner than scheduled, simply because the dependencies have been fulfilled earlier.

Some packages contain a facility called Workload Balancing. This term means that jobs which take a long time to process could be started before jobs of higher priority. To use this facility properly, the latest time a job can finish needs to be established.

If there is a problem with a job, some scheduling packages have the facility to set up the necessary restore job, run that job, and then restart the original job at the right point.

To cope with many problem situations, Ops must have the ability to override the package.

When purchasing a scheduling package check for the following as a minimum:

* how many relationships between jobs are allowed? - some packages may have an upper limit

* which method(s) does the package use to schedule? - some packages may schedule only by Calendar or by Criteria

* does the package support workload balancing?

* what security is included in the package and how many levels of security?

* how are jobs restarted if there is a problem?

* does the package support operator override?

* does the package allow you to model future workloads?

* is the supplier of the package able to train or recommend training on the package?

Why use them?   By using a scheduling package, manual operator intervention is minimal. The workload that the IT system throughputs is improved and the possibility of human error is reduced.

Section 7
Tools

It is recommended that a scheduling package is implemented if any of the following apply or if it is otherwise shown to be cost effective:

* the site is large and/or complex

* the site is moving towards automated/unattended operating

* there are a large number of jobs dependent on each other

* there is, or is going to be, a Bridge set up

* the production work flow is complex and prone to error.

7.2 Magnetic tape and data cartridge management systems

What they do

Tape management packages work with magnetic tapes and data cartridges.

There are several tape management packages; these need to be selected carefully. Their main functions are:

* to provide automated support for tape housekeeping and maintenance, including for example

    - allocating tapes and releasing them for reuse

    - helping to ensure even patterns of use where appropriate

    - constructing and 'triggering' cleaning schedules

    - maintaining life expiry schedules

    - maintaining the security of data

* to help automate archiving (vault management) for offsite storage

* to help identify growth requirements.

Vault management is concerned with controlling the movement of tape cycles from one storage location to another. As a tape cycle is used, the tape management system automatically logs a different vault identifier against each tape.

Tape management packages can be used for data cartridges and these can be used in conjunction with data-cartridge robots. These robots can automatically select the right data cartridge and load it, thereby reducing the operator workload. The robots are now very reliable, but obviously need regular maintenance.

Warning - One problem with tape management packages is their potential vulnerability. If there is a disaster, until the master file for the tape management system has been restored, none of the other restore tapes can be used. Therefore, one of the most protected files in the installation should be this master file.

What to look for

When purchasing a tape management package, check the following, as a minimum:

* how good is the tape protection, against accidental or malicious misuse, provided by the package?

* does the package automatically change the vault identifier as tapes move from one storage location to another?

* how does the package record when tapes are ready for reuse or replacement?

* how easy is it to restore the tape management system?

Why use them?

If a tape management package is used, the tape data is better protected, reducing accidental loss or corruption of data, and the number of manual, error-prone tasks and reruns is reduced.

A tape management package should be purchased if any of the following apply or it can otherwise be shown to be cost effective:

* a large quantity of tapes is used at the site, eg 2000 or more

* the site has a Bridge set up or the tape devices are separate from the console operators

* the site is considering unattended/automated operating

* the movement of tapes from the site to offsite storage is complex.

Section 7
Tools

7.3 Disk management systems

What they do

Various disk management packages are available, covering all aspects of the management of disk volumes. The suppliers of the CPU and disk drives should be consulted as to the applicability of these packages, as the facilities could be provided as standard (eg within the operating system).

The operation of disk management packages requires that they take account of a range of factors such as retention period, recovery, space fragmentation, disk overflow, file and record activity levels, and channel use. Some packages merely report against values or thresholds set; but increasingly they invoke corrective action. The corrective action may be, for instance, file and disk reorganization or file and data archiving.

A common feature is the archiving of under-used data files to tape to utilize space on a disk better.

What to look for

When purchasing a disk management package, check the following, as a minimum:

* how good is the disk protection (eg against accidental or malicious misuse) within the package?

* does the package automatically release, archive and restore under-used files?

Why use them?

If a disk management package is used, the constant monitoring and actioning of requests for disk space can be minimized. The need for job control conversions may be eliminated because of device independence - it becomes unnecessary to specify the disk volume on which a file is (to be) placed. Disk space may be collectively pooled and unused space constantly reclaimed.

A disk management package should be purchased if any of the following apply or if it can otherwise be shown to be cost effective:

* the site has a continual lack of disk space

* there is, or is going to be, a Bridge set up

* the site is considering unattended/automated operating

* the site has a large and/or complex disk installation

* disk space is regularly over allocated
* important files are used only occasionally
* disk management is a manual time-consuming task.

Disk management packages may not be needed if existing operating system software already does the job well.

7.4 JCL validation and management systems

What they do

Software packages exist that check syntax and spelling in job control programs. Some of these packages also have the facility to do a dummy run to ensure that the job control program is accessing valid filenames. Ensuring that the job control program is correct before application testing begins can save an organization time in getting the application accepted for live running. The packages can be run either in batch mode or online, and can provide the job documentation that cross references programs, libraries, datasets and procedures.

What to look for

When purchasing the job control package, check the following, as a minimum:

* does the package validate the job control?
* does the package produce job stream documentation (ie all the documentation required to enable the operators to run jobs)?

Why use them?

By using a job control management package, errors are eliminated, which saves on CPU resource by reducing reruns, and staff resource by saving time on debugging job control. These packages also help keep job documentation up to date and facilitate the production of up-to-date error-free job control listings.

A job control package should be purchased if any of the following apply or it can otherwise be shown to be cost effective:

* there are lots of reruns caused by job control errors
* there is, or is planned, a Bridge
* the site is considering unattended/automated operating
* the site is a large and/or complex installation.

7.5 Job documentation systems

What they do
Job documentation packages produce job and suite documentation (including flowcharts) and generally allow this documentation to be updated online. These packages frequently allow for management information to be provided, eg compare size of programs.

What to look for
When purchasing a job documentation package, check the following, as a minimum:

* does the package produce job and suite flowcharts?
* can the documentation be changed online?

Why use them?
If a job documentation package is used, the accuracy and consistency of the documentation is improved. With automation of a traditionally time-consuming activity, both staff resources and time are saved. This saving increases the productivity of the IT organization.

A job documentation package should be purchased if any of the following apply or if it can otherwise be shown to be cost effective:

* job documentation is often out of date
* the site has, or is planning, a Bridge
* the site is considering unattended/automated operations
* the site is a large and/or complex installation.

7.6 Output and distribution systems

What they do
Output and distribution packages control output production and distribution from the moment the output is planned to the time the user receives the print. The criteria the packages work on need to be set up first, eg define who receives the report and how much of the report the user gets.

The main functions are:

* the report can be limited to the parts wanted by the user
* multiple copies of the entire report or of selected sections can be produced

* reports are grouped by recipient within delivery location

* reports for each job are spooled as a group when the job is complete

* the number of whole reports and individual pages received by each recipient are recorded; this information can be updated and queried online

* report production can be monitored and managed efficiently.

What to look for

When purchasing an output and distribution package, check the following, as a minimum:

* does the package allow parts of reports to be printed?

* does the package track the status (eg queued, printing) of reports?

* can the reports be viewed online?

* does the package archive report files?

* does the package work on the printers installed at the site?

* what charging capabilities does it have?

* what security facilities does the package support?

Why use them?

By using an output distribution package, the staff can ensure that the reports are delivered to the correct person at the correct location. Paper, time and computer resource are saved as the users can get only the parts of reports that they need and can also view the reports online. Packages can limit the number of pages to be printed, in accordance with the contents of SLAs. Reports can be tracked from the time they are created to the time they are delivered to the user, allowing good security monitoring.

An output distribution package should be purchased if any of the following apply or it can otherwise be shown to be cost effective:

* users are in charge of their own output

* the site has a Bridge set up

* the site is considering unattended/automated operations

Section 7
Tools

- full reports are not needed on paper
- the distribution process is complex and reports 'get lost'
- suites produce output for many sites and any site has many reports from different suites
- output handling is time consuming
- the site is a large and/or complex installation.

7.7 Console operator automation systems

What they do

Console operator automation systems provide automated support for many of the activities of console operators. For example, the systems suppress many of the messages that appear on the master console and provide pre-programmed replies to known intervention messages; they allow time dependent commands to be initiated automatically.

What to look for

A console operator automation package should ideally be able to interface with all systems and subsystems that can potentially issue messages to the console; eg network, database, scheduler, tape/disk management systems.

The package should be table driven as far as possible to allow for ease of maintenance and quick implementation. It is also more likely to be used by Ops if to implement the package a complex programming language does not have to be learned.

The package should provide full and comprehensive Help facilities. Although messages are suppressed from appearing on the console they should still be recorded to the system log for later investigation if needed.

Why use them?

These packages offer the following benefits:

- the operators are more likely to notice essential messages, since the number of non-essential messages to the console is reduced
- potential for mistakes is reduced, and speed of processing improved, by the use of pre-programmed replies to expected operator intervention messages
- being able to interface with many (sub)systems provides the opportunity for 'console consolidation' leading to a more manageable environment - provides the physical basis of a Bridge setup

The IT Infrastructure Library
Computer Operations Management

* critical tasks, for example network start-up, can be initiated on time even if the operators are doing something else

* standard operational procedures can be implemented and incident handling can be managed in a more timely and consistent manner, thus improving management control

* operator productivity and system availability are improved.

Annex A. Glossary of terms

Acronyms and abbreviations used in this module

CCTA	Central Computer and Telecommunications Agency
CPU	Central Processing Unit
CRAMM	CCTA Risk Analysis and Management Method
FEP	Front End Processor
I/O	Input/Output
IPL	Initial Program Load
IS	Information Systems
IT	Information Technology
JCL	Job Control Language
MOD	Ministry of Defence
OSG	Operations Support Group
PC	Personal Computer
PDU	Power Distribution Unit
PRINCE	Projects in Controlled Environments
PTF	Program Temporary Fixes
RCF	Run Control File
SLA	Service Level Agreement
SLR	Service Level Requirement
TP	Transaction Processing
VAT	Value Added Tax

Definitions used in this module

Advanced operations A computer operations function in which the advances in hardware and software have been utilized to allow more automated control, releasing Ops personnel to take on more technical roles such as that of operations analysts.

The IT Infrastructure Library
Computer Operations Management

Automated operating
A mode of operating computers in which the processes have been designed to minimize the need for human intervention (eg automated responses to set console messages).

Bridge
See **Operations Bridge**.

Console consolidation
The control of IT services by using one, or a small number of consoles located centrally (where a large number of consoles, often geographically dispersed, have been used previously for that purpose). This technique is particularly useful when running IT services using an Operations Bridge.

Greenfield site
An IT facility, planned or newly installed, which does not replace an existing facility in the organization or location concerned.

Lights-out operating
Otherwise known as darkroom operating, is where the computer room is not staffed, but people are available to control the system via one or more terminals or consoles located nearby, often as part of an Operations Bridge. Normally this mode of operating entails devices that require attention being separately located from the central computer hardware. Typically this will involve large printers or tapedecks etc being located in a separate room, or equipment such as local printers being dispersed among the users on a 'self-service' basis.

Operability standard
A standard laid down to help ensure application software and other items of the IT infrastructure are produced in a way that makes Computer Operations more efficient.

Operations analyst
An operator with sufficient experience and breadth of knowledge to be capable of performing duties, in support of Computer Operations, outside the normal range of operator tasks. Such duties could include tasks associated with, for example, configuration management, operations programming, security, and writing and maintaining JCL. The operations analyst might also represent Computer Operations on applications development project boards.

Operations Bridge
The combination, in one physical location, of Computer Operations, Network Control and the Help Desk. See also **Lights-out operating**.

Operations Support Group (OSG)
A group of people that supports Ops on technical matters, for example, by providing and maintaining Ops standards, documentation, tools, and the interface between Ops and the rest of IT infrastructure management. A typical OSG is staffed by operations analysts.

Annex A
Glossary of terms

PRINCE An enhanced version of PROMPT, this is the method adopted within government for planning, managing and controlling IS projects. It provides guidance on the management components (organization, plans and controls) and on the technical components (end products and the activities needed to produce them).

Service Level Agreement (SLA) The written agreement or 'contract' between the users and the IT service provider which documents the agreed service levels for an IT service. Typically it will cover: service hours, service availability, user support levels, throughputs and terminal response times, restrictions, functionality and the service levels to be provided in a contingency. It may also include security and accounting policy.

Unattended operating Unattended operating has developed into a generic term describing a range of modes of operating computers where operators are not present in the same room as the equipment. In the following list, all but the first have an element of unattended operating: fully-staffed operating; lights-out/Bridge operating; remote operating; exception operating; completely unattended operating.

Annex B. Example - Job descriptions

NOTE! These are example job descriptions and will need to be adapted according to organizations' particular requirements.

B1 Ops Manager

Responsibilities

Setting up and managing a computer operation, supported by other IT infrastructure management disciplines, that is responsible for operating computers in such a way that IT services can be delivered to the level of quality required in the Service Level Agreements. The operation must be able also to absorb change at a rate consistent with the business need.

Possible mission statement

To set up and manage an efficient computer operation that is capable of delivering, with support from other IT infrastructure management functions, IT services to the quality required in the Service Level Agreements, whilst absorbing change at a rate consistent with business needs.

Key objectives

To:

* direct and administer the Ops-area production process to meet production targets

* develop and maintain controls and procedures to ensure that the Ops production process runs efficiently; to ensure in the event of failure that Ops can recover the operation in accordance with a predefined and tested recovery or contingency plan, to maintain an agreed fallback level of service within a set time

* ensure that Ops staff are managed effectively to allow production targets to be met (in a shift pattern if needed) and that these staff have up-to-date job descriptions, are regularly appraised, and have a current training plan for personal development; to arrange for the recruitment of staff as necessary

* plan and oversee the installation of computer hardware; to liaise regularly with vendor staff to ensure adequate support is provided

* ensure that the physical environment is maintained and secure according to contractual requirements and business needs

* ensure that the Ops budget is managed within the financial limits agreed

The IT Infrastructure Library
Computer Operations Management

* ensure that new production systems meet the agreed operability criteria for live running prior to accepting them for running

* ensure that the IT Services Manager is provided with regular feedback on Ops performance

* ensure that all contractual documentation relevant to maintenance contracts is complete.

Dimensions — These vary according to site; should include staff supervised, amount of budget administered/responsible for, typical hours of work.

Organization — See section 3.3.2 for details of a typical Ops organization.

B2 Shift Leader

Responsibilities — Managing the Ops activities on a day-to-day shift basis, ensuring that the agreed production targets are met.

Key objectives — To:

* direct Ops staff to run the computer production cycle in line with the controls and processes established to meet production deadlines, to ensure that there is an effective handover with other shifts in order to maintain the level of IT services across shift boundaries

* ensure, with Problem Management/specialist support/vendor assistance as required, that incidents arising from or impacting the production cycle have minimum effect and are resolved within the target timeframe. To ensure all such incidents are documented according to the defined problem management procedures and to ensure any computer system changes proposed to resolve incidents and problems are subject to change management control

* provide regular feedback on Ops performance to the Ops Manager, recommending any improvements required

* ensure that system and environmental housekeeping procedures and system backups are performed to the prescribed standard

* look after Ops personnel matters, including performance reviews and appraisals, disciplinary and training counselling

* assist and deputize for the Ops Manager as required.

Annex B
Example - Job descriptions

Dimensions These vary according to site; should include staff supervised, amount of budget administered/responsible for, typical hours of work.

B3 Senior Operator/Operator

(The roles of senior computer operator and of operator are broadly the same - the difference is in experience, length of service, responsibility, and number of staff)

Responsibilities Undertaking the processing of computer production work to meet the targets set.

Key objectives To:

* carry out the required loading of system software to allow the computers to be used for production and test work

* ensure that workloads are run, by Ops, correctly and on schedule, with the minimum of supervision

* ensure (within the bounds of Ops' overall responsibility) that the computer systems, including hardware, software and applications, always support efficient IT operations, and failing this either

  - identify and analyse any faults and take corrective action or

  - ensure that correct incident reporting is done to allow third party assistance

  using the problem management system in either case

* supervise junior staff in the operation of equipment and train them in the use of such equipment

* ensure that all computer equipment is cleaned according to the cleaning schedule, and perform regular checks on the environmental conditions

* assist and deputize for the shift leader as required.

Dimensions These vary according to site: should include staff supervised, amount of budget administered/responsible for, typical hours of work.

B4 Junior/Trainee Operator

Responsibilities   Operating computer equipment under the close supervision of senior staff and assisting in other operational tasks whilst learning more advanced operating techniques.

Key objectives   To:

* operate computer equipment as directed by senior staff to aid the production cycle
* carry out basic operating, cleaning and maintenance tasks to the standard laid down in Ops manual
* check the quality of printed output and report any errors to senior staff; to present output to data control for distribution in a controlled and prompt manner
* learn the complete duties of a computer operator in order to become a more valuable member of the staff
* become familiar with the IT equipment, with senior staff's help and through background reading.

Dimensions   These vary according to site: should include staff supervised, amount of budget administered/responsible for, typical hours of work.

B5 Operations Analyst

Responsibilities   Setting up and maintenance of the required environment and standards for operational files and for job control to allow efficient processing; and other activities, varying from organization to organization, concerned with supporting Ops.

Key objectives   Typically to:

* take day-to-day responsibility for Ops software tools ensuring their use is efficient and effective (see section 7 for more details)
* be capable of operations programming (understanding and writing source code and being able to make minor program amendments, writing and amending JCL within pre-defined limits and subject to normal change management control)
* ensure that standards for files and for job control are set up and maintained

Annex B
Example - Job descriptions

* set up and control a process for the management of disk and tape files; to allocate disks and tapes according to standard procedures

* ensure that all new application developments adhere to operability and acceptance standards; to liaise with project teams throughout the life of development projects to this end and to carry out pre-live checks; to report any significant events to the Ops Manager with recommended actions

* ensure that in accordance with the requirements of the Software Control & Distribution Manager both production and test libraries are maintained to allow efficient and secure processing

* design and maintain the production scheduling methods and set up a scheduling guide for data control to maintain on a day-to-day basis

* train operators in new application running and arrange for any training from the application project team; to ensure that sufficient operational documentation is present

* specify, select and manage the use of operational support packages; eg tape/disk management

* perform regular reviews, in collaboration where necessary with other IT groups such as capacity management, of operational production cycle efficiency and advise on required enhancements

* ensure that Ops' disaster recovery plans are maintained in line with the overall contingency plan.

Dimensions These vary according to site: should include staff supervised, amount of budget administered/responsible for, typical hours of work.

B6 Data Control Clerk

Responsibilities The control, to or from the computer room, of the input/output of data and run schedules for the production cycle.

Key objectives To:

* ensure all the day-to-day computer schedules are prepared in line with the scheduling guide and submitted to the computer room

* ensure that the input for computer jobs is collected and entered in accordance with the standards for such data

The IT Infrastructure Library
Computer Operations Management

* distribute output to the user sections in an efficient manner to ensure the correct data is available in line with the agreed service level; to present that output in decollated, collated, or other form as appropriate

* operate and maintain equipment in the data control area, highlight any faults, and correct them if possible (under problem management system control); ensure faults not immediately correctable are logged as incidents and resolved

* liaise with Help Desk staff with regard to specific user requirements for output and where necessary alter schedules or output routines as a result, having obtained the necessary authority for these changes

* liaise as required with the computer room staff in order jointly to plan the input/production/output cycle to best meet the target times; to ensure required amendments to Ops procedures and/or SLAs are submitted to change management.

Dimensions

These vary according to site; should include staff supervised, amount of budget administered/responsible for, typical hours of work.

B7 Media Librarian

Responsibilities

Supply and control of the media necessary for the running of the computer operation.

Key objectives

To:

* order magnetic tapes, diskettes, cartridges, paper, microfiche and other media under the direction of the Ops Manager

* develop and maintain a log system for the recording and usage of all computer media, to ensure adequate, but not wasteful, levels of stock are kept

* issue media as directed or authorized by senior staff or in line with the production or test schedules

* set up and maintain a clear physical identification system for magnetic tapes, cartridges, etc for easy identification

* perform security backups and associated rotation of media, ensuring that the correct backup tapes are in the correct secure environment (eg 'father' onsite, 'grandfather' and copy of 'father' offsite)

Annex B
Example - Job descriptions

    * maintain an out-of-hours media control log that clearly shows usage and authorization

    * keep the media storage areas clean and tidy.

Dimensions — These vary according to site: should include staff supervised, amount of budget administered/responsible for, typical hours of work.

B8 Systems Programmer

Responsibilities — Installing, maintaining and, where appropriate, developing systems software and inhouse utilities, and providing technical support for systems software.

Key objectives — To:

- install, maintain and customize system software as required
- develop system software to provide the fullest benefits for the installation in terms of availability, flexibility, performance and value for money
- develop and maintain inhouse utilities as required
- provide specialist technical support for system software
- participate in the development of procedures, as they apply to systems programming group, relating to change management, problem management, security and documentation standards
- participate in the evaluation of system software and implement such software acquired by the installation
- take part in projects and related ongoing activities with other support groups as required.

May also carry out system tuning, to maintain optimum performance levels at all times, under the control of the Capacity Manager.

Dimensions — These vary according to site: should include staff supervised, amount of budget administered/responsible for, typical hours of work.

Annex C. Example - Operations manual contents

The following documentation should be included in the Ops manual:

* copies of all forms/screen formats used and accompanying procedures for using them
* procedures for using installed hardware
* procedures for running installed system and application software
* procedures for using installed tools and other customized software
* system library details
* SLAs regarding online and batch processing
* emergency and call-out procedures
* computer room layout
* details of installed hardware
* maintenance contracts or suitable extracts
* problem management (including escalation thresholds) and other support contracts
* change management procedures as applicable to Ops
* job descriptions
* disaster recovery procedures as they relate to Ops
* security procedures
* online system procedures
* backup procedures
* procedures for the control and management of accommodation and environment
* input control procedures (including data preparation standards)
* output control (including distribution) procedures
* an overview of the scheduling guide or a guide to using the scheduling software

- * media control and maintenance procedures
- * data and system file management procedures including file allocation standards, file/volume restore procedures
- * installation JCL standards
- * guide to general policy
  - towards business service provision
  - professionalism
  - training and staff development
  - standards applicable to all Ops management disciplines
  - dissemination of information
  - management.

The following application system documentation, for each application, should also be included:

- * personnel contacts
- * system summary
- * system flowcharts
- * preprocessing
  - hardware requirements
  - software requirements
  - files required
  - output produced
  - scheduling required
- * processing
  - start-up procedures
  - processing activities
  - expected console messages
  - exception console messages

Annex C
Example - Operations manual contents

- * postprocessing
  - closedown procedures
  - control instructions
  - printer output setup instructions
  - output offline instructions
  - distribution instructions
- * backup and restart procedures.

Annex D
Example - Staff access levels/zones

Annex D. Example - Staff access levels/zones

The criterion used for judging whether staff require access is simple: do they need access to the area to carry out their day-to-day tasks?

Access levels/zones	Staff authorized for entry
1 General Ops Area	All Ops staff
	Problem management support
	Data Controllers
	IT management
	Help Desk staff
2 Computer Room	Computer operators
	Shift management
	Ops Manager
3 Media Storage Area	Media Librarian
	Shift management
	Ops Manager.

Annex E. Example - Procedures for handling cheques/secure items

Any cheques produced out of office hours must be held on the printer queue until the next day. A backup of the printer queue should be taken and held in the fire-proof safe until the cheques are printed successfully and then it must be erased.

During the day the user section logs the number of the first cheque that is to be printed, and then brings the cheques to the computer section.

The operators print the cheques, using 3 pages for the line-up. If there are problems with the line-up, the user must be informed immediately. Cheques used for line-up must be accounted for.

Immediately after the cheques have been printed, the control totals are printed on ordinary stationery. The user section then checks that all the cheques have been printed and there are no cheques missing. This check has to be performed before the user leaves the operations section.

IT Infrastructure Library
Computer Operations Management

Comments Sheet

CCTA hopes that you find this book both useful and interesting. We will welcome your comments and suggestions for improving it.
Please use this form or a photocopy, and continue on a further sheet if needed.

From:

        Name

        Organization

        Address

re: 1990/OM

        Telephone

COVERAGE
Does the material cover your needs?
If not, then what additional material would you like included.

CLARITY
Are there any points which are unclear?
If yes, please detail where and why.

ACCURACY
Please give details of any inaccuracies found.

If more space is required for these or other comments, please continue overleaf.

IT Infrastructure Library
Computer Operations Management

Comments Sheet

OTHER COMMENTS

Return to: IT Infrastructure Management Services
             Central Computer and Telecommunications Agency
             Gildengate House
             Upper Green Lane
             NORWICH, NR3 1DW

Further information

Further information on the contents of this module can be obtained from:

IT Infrastructure Management Services
CCTA
Gildengate House
Upper Green Lane
NORWICH
NR3 1DW

Telephone 0603 694788
(GTN 3014 - 4788).

The price of this publication has been set to make some contribution to the preparation costs incurred by CCTA.